# The 7 Ke to Tap into the Wealth Inside You

M000192216

"Thank you so much, Cali! You are truly an inspiration, and your business sense (along with knowing everything addiction & recovery like the back of your hand) had me leaving the course just bragging on you, so thank you. Honestly, I'm thinking about what I can take next from you."

*~ Lauren Nicole, A&E's Extreme Interventions*

"I want to thank you again for your help! Literally, almost everything thing you said would happen, HAPPENED. The biggest takeaways for me were, ALWAYS make sure you are prepared, trust your gut instinct, don't get disappointed if the person says no at first, and don't underestimate the power of the bottom line :)"

*~ Eric Peyton,*
*Coach and Personal Trainer to the Stars*

"After intensive virtual classroom training with Cali Estes, I, along with several other professional football players and baseball players, have been sought after to coach everyone from corporate elites, to pro athletes and suburban soccer dads. Cali's Pro Training offers the trainees a roadmap to help clients reach their ultimate goal, and her approach meets you right where you are. She's a leader and is on the front line of an ever-changing world. Thanks Cali, you are the future of educating the world!... I'm glad to call you Coach!"

*~ Vance Johnson, Denver Broncos (#82) and*
*CEO of The Vance Johnson Recovery Center*

"I was amazed at the amount of valuable information, helpful strategies, and tips that were presented. I warmly recommend you!"

*~ James M. Michie, CEO, Sweeden*

"I enjoyed this! My goal is to gain more knowledge and have resources in the states that I can feed leads to from my place here in Mexico! Just to make sure I'm referring people to the right sources so we can maximize the success of what we're doing here! Value Added, that's our goal! Thanks So Much, very impressed with your knowledge, You Got This!"

*~ Roy Moffi, Hotel B &B Owner, Mexico*

"Cali Estes is a dynamic, informed, and energetic instructor who knows her stuff. Rarely am I engaged by a speaker or instructor, but Cali had me sitting on the edge of my seat for two full days of training. I also took 26 pages of notes! The class was interactive, included homework, and created a community of individuals previously not connected. Thank you, Cali, for setting the bar!"

*~ Jean Krisle, Founder 10,000 Beds, Inc.*

"I like the guidance and feedback, interaction, and various methodologies of other Coaches. Also, it was a pleasure being amongst those with a common cause. The course offered insight into addictive behaviors and best approach for communication and understanding of first contact."

*~ Gloria Grant, Connecting Roots, LLC*

"Hey Cali! I've been reading *The Millionaire Mind,* and one of the exercises was to reach out to someone you know who is very successful and whom you admire. You came to mind.

Here's what I admire and inspires me about you and your example:

- you are driven and committed to your dreams and helping others
- you don't let others opinion of you distract you from your vision
- you live a life that is authentic to you and your dreams, while still being of service and living within society in your own way
- you make a lot of money and are still of service in a big way – thanks for the example that both are possible!
- you are available to anyone – not just those on the 'same level'
- you are expanding in new directions consistently, and you aren't afraid to try something new
- you are compassionate, but also have a good sense for b.s. and won't allow it to slide
- It's inspiring to know all this is possible!"

*~ Dylan Lungren*

"Cali recharges batteries, her training and education is awesome."

*~ Eric Lapp, CEO, The Raleigh House of Hope*

"I found class to be imperative to honing in skills taught by Cali in the live classes. We were able to discuss live case studies, get different viewpoints, and run over other areas we might have needed help with. The weekly meetings hold a safe place where everyone can come together to discuss what they need."

*~ Alexis Jonson, Author, Star of A&E's Narcoland, and Playboy Playmate*

"I initially reached out to Dr. Estes because my facility was experiencing high AMA rates. We were admitting roughly 30 patients each month, and, on average, 13 were leaving early, against staff advice. As a result, our average length of stay was only 16 days, and our census was stuck around 18 out of 32 beds. Within 2 months of hiring Dr. Cali, we have increased our length of stay to 26 days, and we have reduced the number of patients leaving early against staff advice from 13 to 4 per month. As a result of these changes and some additional marketing strategies she implemented for us, I am happy to say we have increased our census from 18 to 32, and we now have a waiting list. Dr. Estes is professional, detail-oriented, and able to focus on what matters to drive results."

*~ Matt Boyle, Vice President of Finance, Landmark Senior Living Communities*

# The 7 Key Principles to Tap into the Wealth Inside You

*How to Unpause Your Life and
Make Success a Reality*

*Dr. Cali Estes*

CHECKMATE PRESS
checkmatepress.com

Copyright © 2020 by **Dr. Cali Estes**

All rights reserved. No part of this publication may be reproduced, distributed, or transmitted in any form or by any means without prior written permission.

**Checkmate Press books are published by:**

**McLean Media Group, LLC**
**4364 Glenwood Dr**
**Bozeman, Montana 59718 USA**
**www.checkmatepress.com**

**The 7 Key Principles to Tap into the Wealth Inside You /**
**Dr. Cali Estes. -- 1st ed.**
ISBN 978-1-7321781-3-7

The Publisher has strived to be as accurate and complete as possible in the creation of this book.

This book is not intended for use as a source of legal, business, accounting, or financial advice. All readers are advised to seek services of competent professionals in legal, business, accounting, and finance field.

In practical advice books, like anything else in life, there are no guarantees of income or results made. Readers are cautioned to rely on their own judgment about their individual circumstances to act accordingly.

While all attempts have been made to verify information provided in this publication, the Publisher assumes no responsibility for errors, omissions, or contrary interpretation of the subject matter herein. Any perceived slights of specific persons, peoples, or organizations are unintentional.

# TABLE OF CONTENTS

# FOREWORD

"You'd best un-fuck yourself right now, son!"
—The drill instructor from *Full Metal Jacket.*

Those words always stuck with me. There's something to be said for feeling like you're fucked. You're sitting still while the rest of the world is blowing past you at a hundred miles an hour. It's a horrible feeling.

Unfortunately, it's a feeling we live with far too often. Whether through problems at work, at home, financial, emotional, or otherwise, we spend way too much time feeling stuck, and not enough time working on improving ourselves, so we don't.

I've started and sold three companies, I've written five books, all bestsellers, I've been at the top of my game more times than most people ride in an elevator. But I've also been on the bottom. I've seen it from both sides, and let me tell you, the bottom is a lot less fun. The bottom is also scary as hell.

Imagine swimming away from the shore, and once out there, you realize that there's a current pushing you further and further away from land. Scary, huh? While you're looking at where you are, you're being pulled further and further out. How do you start making your way back to shore without drowning? It can feel impossible.

Feelings that fester inside can gnaw at us and prevent us from reaching our potential. This, in turn, can cause more feelings of inadequacy, and the cycle continues, with no visible way out. It's crappy, to say the least.

But there *is* a way out. Dr. Cali Estes lays it out in the following pages, in a no bullshit, no buzzwords way, as only she can. The hundreds of people who have benefited from her teachings are living proof that this system works. It's possible to regain your power, to regain control of your life, to move on from that which is holding you back.

It's possible because I've seen it happen. If you're ready to move on, if you're ready to grow, if you're ready to un-fuck yourself, I encourage you to give this book a shot. Dr. Cali knows from what she speaks.

Unpause your life. Start now. What are you waiting for?

Peter Shankman
Author, Entrepreneur, Keynote Speaker
www.FasterThanNormal.com
October 16th, 2019
New York, NY/Abu Dhabi, UAE

# INTRODUCTION

Do you feel like your life is on pause, somewhat stuck? Do you desperately desire to find a way to move forward, to find the wealth and success that you know is somewhere deep inside you?

I can't think of anyone who hasn't had this happen to them. At some point in your life, it's natural to get stuck, feel like you are floundering about, confused about the next steps to take, maybe you even feel lost.

Or maybe something has happened in your life, the loss of a loved one or a job. Or possibly you have found yourself becoming bored, disinterested, or even frustrated by your current path. We used to call it a 'midlife crisis,' but it seems to be happening earlier and earlier in our lives.

Like many of my clients, maybe an addiction, substance abuse, or an issue surrounding your life that has intervened, knocking you off the course you were on. Unfortunately, too many people find themselves in this predicament.

Wouldn't you want to find a way to get unstuck, to unpause your life, and move confidently towards the success you desire, the success you know waits for you that you feel you don't know how to access?

Have you noticed that certain people seem to have all the luck, or what you think is luck? They get a great job, and they have a beautiful house, their spouse or significant other seems perfect on paper. They never seem to have a shitty thing happen ever.

They boast about it on social media, and their lives seem picture-perfect. Well, maybe occasionally they get a flat tire. But they always seem to be sipping on a Mai Tai somewhere in Cancun and having a great life. You know, just as much as they do, you work just as hard as they are. You want to get ahead, you want to win, and yet you feel stuck.

Despite your best efforts to get ahead of the game, to find the best path for your desired joy and happiness, the world keeps sending you challenges or roadblocks to keep you stuck. You seem to be in a perpetual holding pattern, never moving up.

How many times have you seen others living a life that seems completely ideal? They have the perfect job and make plenty of money, they are in a wonderful relationship and have loads of fantastic friends. It's like everything they touch turns to gold.

Have you ever felt ashamed of your job or financial situation? Are you tired of having more month than a paycheck?

Do you struggle with your health or relationships? Are you challenged by substance abuse, constant stress or worry, and just generally feeling like crap?

You probably hear that you need to hustle and grind or maybe that you need to get a good job, a good spouse, or a new car, and you will be happy.

There are a lot of myths, misconceptions, and also a lot of misinformation out there about what it takes to find your true calling, your real purpose in life, and reach a level of success you never thought you could attain.

Financial achievement and career fulfillment, along with relationship satisfaction, may seem like luck or being born into the right situation or being at the right place at the right time, am I right? But it isn't always this way, and I am here to teach you a different way.

You can have everything you want that you thought you could never attain. I, for one, grew up poor with no contacts and no wealthy friends. And I work with CEO's, executives, high-level musicians, actors, and professional athletes.

I cracked the code, and I'm going to teach you how to do it too. It is essential to finding happiness and satisfaction in your life. Finding this key not only affects you but everyone around you.

Maybe you've even tried everything you can think of, like a new diet, a new job, or a new relationship. Perhaps you've been to rehab, counseling, or therapy. And maybe you've been to a doctor who prescribed medications for your anxiety or depression.

You've tried everything you can think of, some things your friends and family told you would work, and even some stuff the professionals prescribed or recommended.

Nothing happened.

And it never will happen if you keep trying to play the game that way.

You are most definitely not alone. Millions of others have experienced the same thing. They think that if they have the right job, the right partner, the right opportunity things will turn around, and then they will be living the life they deserve, the life they desire.

They are feeling stuck in their shitty job, their unsatisfactory relationship, and they think they are in a rut they can't get out of. I call this the "hamster wheel." They want health, happiness, and success, but they can't seem to get off the hamster wheel and find the right path to get there.

When you think about it, the world has changed. No longer do people spend years at the same job, accumulating a pension and healthy retirement. The average length of stay for someone between the ages of 25 to 34 is about three years, less than the time it takes to get a college degree or serve in the military. (I never lasted longer than one year at any job I've had.)

Single income families are scarce, and over three-quarters of families in the U.S. have both parents working while attempting to juggle the kids and the finances. And at the same time, relatively speaking, we are making less money.

Divorce rates are high, and addiction to drugs and alcohol is at record levels as people attempt to escape the challenges and anxieties which fuel their depression.

There has been a decrease in life expectancy in the U.S. due to addiction and a decline in the emotional wellbeing of Americans. It is scary to realize that these issues have been significant enough to drag down the entire country's average length of life.

It's all hustle, hustle, go, go, go all the time, and we rarely sit down to have a meal with our families anymore. And if we do, we end up playing on our phones. We endure constant bombardment with media and social media, telling us what we need to buy or where we need to go to be happy, or which pill we need to take to be satisfied, which gets us to spend money we don't even have.

People don't know who they should be, what they should be doing, or who they should look to for support anymore. And they are afraid to leave their current situation despite its negative impact on their health and finances due to FEAR.

The number of people who say they are happy is less than 1 in 3 Americans as we continue to face contentious issues and the challenges of life.

I'll put it to you straight up, you've created this life, this one *you created,* with which you are not so happy. But there's good news. You always have the option to create a new one. It seems simple, right? Well, it is. Given the right tools and mindset, anybody can create the life they want. So, how do you do it?

The real problem is a lack of direction. Most people have a hard time finding a path they desire and a course they are satisfied with, and they find they have somehow managed to make choices and decisions that make them less than happy. You are stuck, and you wonder, "How did I get here?" Maybe you got married young, had kids, and you are sitting on the sofa trying to figure out where it went wrong. Is that you?

Maybe you're starting your life over. You just got divorced, you're in your 40's, and you don't know where to turn. Despite having to learn to "swipe right" or "swipe left," starting over is hard at any age, but learning a whole new way of doing it can be challenging.

A lot of my clients experience these two scenarios. They have been in the same relationship, at the same job, and done the same thing for a long time, and they are bored. Maybe they have the perfect house, the ideal wife, the kids, the dog, the white picket fence, and they don't know what to do, they feel that life is just passing by them. The question, "Is the grass greener on the other side?" lurks in their minds. "What am I missing out on?" is another common stumbling block or the constant obsession, "Maybe life would be more exciting if…" Hence the mid-life crisis of fast cars, boobs jobs, and stay-at-home housewives suddenly becoming strippers.

Or, many of my other clients are a little younger and feel lost, not wanting to buy things, but have experiences they can remember years down the line. This group is perfectly happy living in an RV and not working full time, but still wants their $7.00 Starbucks specialty whip coffee. They want to obtain the best salary while working the least amount of hours, and still having a sense of purpose in life, but they feel lost. Some of them may be 35 years old and still live at home, "trying to find themselves."

Neither group is focused, and both groups are constantly seeking something to fulfill them, yet they are not sure what that something is.

Because without a focus on a desired goal and acceptance of things outside of our control, it's easy to become distracted and disinterested. Previous choices seem less attractive when the new, shiny option is in front of us.

This "grass is greener syndrome" often causes everyone to quickly switch jobs, relationships, and cars as they continually chase the things they think are going to make them happy and successful. Yet these seekers still feel a void.

The not-so-real images, videos, and comments on social media don't help and have been proven to increase depression. When people are constantly checking their feeds and see everyone #winning, while they feel like their world is just a mess, it leads to unrealistic expectations and disappointment.

This constant "Keep Up With The Joneses" mentality leads people to compare their life to what they are seeing on social media, which is most likely not a reflection of what's going on. Just because Becky posts pictures of herself in a bikini at the beach does not mean she's having fun. We don't see the rainstorm that moved in later or the kids having a meltdown over ice cream cones.

That's why it seems like there is no clear way to get out of the trap many people feel they have landed in, this feeling of being stuck with no way out.

But it doesn't have to be this way. **If you are ready to discover your authentic self, to find your correct path to happiness and success, then keep reading.** No matter your situation, no matter how negative it seems right now, you can pull yourself out of it, I've seen it countless times.

I'm about to show you how to take advantage of a system I call *Unpause Your Life*. This system will help you create your perfect vision for the life you truly desire and give you the roadmap to get there.

It's a strategy that I've taught hundreds of times with tremendous success. It has aided people from all walks of life who are experiencing massive loss and struggle to get up and thrive when they are down and out, at their lowest point. And I'm confident it will work for you.

You must realize that we all have limitless potential and can overcome anything by changing the script we are following. It's a bit like a movie, you know how it starts, you understand the middle, and you know the ending.

For example, nearly every 14-year-old girl, at one time (except for me), dreams of their wedding dress. They dream of their wedding day. They write the script for their perfect and most beautiful day. They imagine getting married, and having a family is going to be amazing.

Fast forward, and they have a five-year-old and seven-year-old fighting over a truck while they are changing a diaper with one hand, a phone in the other, as their dinner burns on the stove. They struggle to make ends meet, and they hate their lives. Why? The script has changed, desires have changed. So many get written into a story they don't like.

I'm here to say, "Don't give up! You don't have to settle for anything less than what you want!"

You can sit in it and wallow in misery, or you can take action. You can't get caught up in your head. You are going to have to get on your feet and act and get moving.

> YOU HAVE UNTAPPED, LIMITLESS POTENTIAL. YOU WILL SUCCEED IF YOU FIND THE CLARITY AND TRULY BELIEVE YOU CAN ACHIEVE YOUR DREAMS, AND YOU PUT IN THE WORK.

In his New Thought Movement book, William Walker Atkinson used the phrase Thought Vibration or the Law of Attraction in the Thought World (1906), stating that "like attracts like."

Without even knowing it, I became a practitioner of the New Thought Movement at an early age. Let me explain a little by giving you a short history of my background.

I was born and grew up in Pottstown, Pennsylvania, which is basically a ghetto about forty minutes west of Philadelphia.

I have no fond memories of my childhood. I wish I had a few, but I don't. My Mom made minimum wage at a job she had since her teen years, and we were pretty much broke all the time, eating frozen TV dinners, hot dogs, and shit-on-a-shingle for supper.

My Dad was a total hustler. He ran a car dealership, a gas station, a gun shop, a real estate office, a bunch of "businesses."

But he never brought the cash home for us, it always went to whomever his current "young-chick-of-the-day" was, and there were a lot of them.

My childhood was not great, by any means, and you can read all the gory details in my other book, *I Married A Junkie*. Anyway, I found myself highly motivated to get the hell out of there. I began saving money for college when I was eight or so because I knew that could be my ticket out.

I also found myself a young entrepreneur. I used to throw talent shows with the neighbor kids and charge the parents to get in. I would bake and sell my cookies and cakes. I even created a newsletter and sold that.

Until recently, I believed I had succeeded in my efforts to move away from Pottstown and build a successful career and beautiful marriage through guts, determination, and hard work.

And this is something you hear all the time. Hustle, hustle, and grind, and you'll make it big. Oh, and follow your passion too.

What if I told you there was a way to bypass the hustle and grind? And that after you find yourself, you will also find your purpose.

Then the work hardly seems like work and everything falls into place.

This "end-around" doesn't rely on you working your fingers to the bone or waiting around until your true calling reveals itself.

Finding your passion is not the goal.

The real goal should be finding your deepest desire.

You see, that's what made the Law of Attraction work for me when I wanted out of Pottstown. I desired to be anywhere but there, and the Law worked to make sure that happened.

However, it's not enough to have the desire. It's to focus on it so entirely that you begin to picture the steps it will take to get there, and then start taking those steps.

I wanted out of P-town, I knew that college would do that, I needed money for college, I sold cookies to my friends.

This focus on actions to bring your desire to fruition is what most people who talk about the Law of Attraction miss. It's like they think by wanting money and staring at a $100 bill or writing themselves a check it's all just going to fall in their lap. A lot of times you'll hear people say, I want to win the lottery! And they'll buy one ticket. That's not how it works. It's more than just setting the intention. It's also about the law of averages and a lot of work.

The Principles I outline in this book, and the simple steps I encourage you to take with each of them will almost certainly guarantee you will find your desired outcome. But, you must put in the effort to get there.

Before you can take advantage of the 7 Principles, you may need to change the way you think about the Law of Attraction. Hoping and wishing will only create disappointment in your world.

It doesn't work like that. We need to take action steps to find out who you are, what you should be doing, and who you should be with along the way.

What if you focus on the wins and not the losses? So many of us get hooked on our failures. We get stuck on those things that take us down the wrong path, and one loss becomes another loss and another... focus on the wins.

You are going to need to adjust your attitude about money and your perceptions of reality, which may be limiting you.

Someone once told me, "Attitude is everything." I think they may be right! I believe we are all capable of success with the right attitude.

I hope you can see by now that there is no good reason for you not to be enjoying success within all aspects of your life. If you apply the principles I'm about to share with you, in as little as one day, you should start seeing and feeling the results. At a bare minimum, you will be more in-tune with yourself and know who you are, which is the ultimate foundation to begin the journey towards your purpose, your tribe, and more money.

But you won't want to stop there, because once you see how these Principles work for you the first time through, you will be able to apply them to any desire, anytime, to build the life of your dreams.

# CHAPTER ONE

# CREATING AND SUSTAINING THE ENERGY NEEDED

*Eat Your Broccoli*

"Are Pop-Tarts® healthy?"

I wasn't surprised to learn that this is the number one search term for this sugar-packed, processed dessert that passes for food in some circles.

I am always telling my clients, "Pop-Tarts® are not a breakfast food."

Constantly. It's a mantra of sorts.

Before you can begin to find the desired results in your life that will lead to your version of "success," you must treat your body and your mind with respect, kindness, and care.

This concept is our First Principle of Success and will be critical in helping you create and maintain the energy you need and have available if you want it. Your success is going to hinge directly upon how you take care of yourself. Your body and brain are extraordinary gifts most of us take for granted.

Your physical and mental performance levels depend entirely upon the chemicals you ingest. High performers also rely on consistent brain and body fitness behaviors as well.

Let's talk first about what you are eating and drinking, or other substances you may also be introducing into your system.

If you have taken any basic chemistry classes in high school, or even watched the Mentos® and Coke® videos, you understand that when you mix certain chemicals, you get specific reactions.

Your body is just a large set of ongoing chemical reactions, all day every day. Without going too deep into how it all works, your cells are using different chemicals to produce energy and to work with each other, keeping you alive, moving, and thinking clearly.

When you put good chemicals into your body, you are going to get the best reactions and the best performance you can hope for from your cells.

When you eat food-like products full of bad chemicals instead of real food, well, you are going to get reactions and performance levels that are less than ideal, erratic, and possibly damaging, especially over the long-term. Your body and brain are very resilient and can recover from a lot of abuse and neglect, but only for a while.

Where do you think Pop-Tarts® fall if we think of them as a chemical? Good or bad? You're right if you choose option B: pure and total crap. Food is made up of chemicals, that's all it is. If you wanted to analyze an almond, it would be broken down into its chemical components.

The way I see it, a meal contains real, whole food. Items without a list of ingredients on the back. Carrots, salmon, apples, macadamia nuts, things like this. Nothing added, no processing except for some cleaning, maybe a little roasting or cooking.

Anything that is not a meal, or part of a meal, is either a snack or dessert. Snacks are things that contain real, whole foods, like a meal does, but are more like multiple layers of whole foods. Carrots with hummus would be a snack.

"Dessert" is anything that's in a can, a bag, or processed in some way. Real, whole food is in its natural state. "Dessert" has been processed and changed around or contains ingredients that have been altered from their natural state. Chips are a dessert, not a snack, and so are cookies and cake.

And if for some reason you are still wondering, dessert is not good for you. There's a difference between food and "food-like product." I have all my clients shop around the perimeter of the grocery store. This area in any grocery is where you will find food — meats, vegetables, fruit, foods that often come without a list of ingredients, right. "Food-like product" is found in the center of the store. Things like Doritos®. Not food.

~

**DO THIS:** Look in your pantry and your refrigerator, what percentage of your food is not real? If it's like most grocery stores, it will be about 85% processed dessert items. If it has a list of ingredients you cannot pronounce, it is not real food.

Need a food mood journal? Head over to www.UnpauseYourlife.com for your FREE copy!

Go shopping and replace what isn't real, whole food. You can't have the bad stuff around, or you will continue to eat it. If you feel bad about throwing it away, donate it to a neighbor or the food pantry.

~

If you add drugs or alcohol on top of poor food choices, this will only help you feel better temporarily. Sugar and cocaine have the same effect on your brain, "pinging" or stimulating it the same, encouraging the release of dopamine and serotonin. The withdrawal for sugar and heroin are the same, their chemical make-up being nearly identical.

Again, these are chemicals reacting in a certain way within your body and brain, masking pain or anxiety, satisfying a craving, and creating a false sense of euphoria. This euphoria only lasts briefly. However, the effect of over-indulgence of certain food-like products can be life-long. Diabetes, high blood pressure, hypertension, MS symptoms, and more are generally avoidable.

I have a client that was diagnosed with multiple sclerosis almost ten years ago. I took her to a naturopath who, among other things, took her off of all sugar and flour. Her symptoms are all in remission, and the lesions in her brain have shrunk. Food is medicine.

Unfortunately, in my line of work, I see the long-term effects of substance abuse daily, and it is not pretty. I once had a client who came to me, claiming he had the cure for alcoholism. It was in a book he had which encouraged a "naltrexone cure." The book was dog-eared and highlighted. I asked him if he had been drinking wine while reading it, and he said, "Yes."

Obviously, there is no 'alcohol cure,' especially when you are reading about it while ingesting the substance.

Even though we know on a cognitive level there are things we should not put into our bodies, we cannot stop. We cannot escape reality. Addiction is a cycle. It's not just drugs and alcohol; it is sugar, sodas, and even energy drinks. Anyone can have a vice.

I love working with people in active addiction and with those who have conquered their addictions. Research tells us that 1 in 5 people have an addiction, but my personal experience shows me that it is closer to 3 in 5. How can that be? Many bad habits are socially acceptable such as food or sugar.

This motivates me, and it helps drive me to continue my mission to guide people like yourself to a newer, better reality because it is out there for you, as long as you want it. You have to take the bull by the horns and go for a run.

Now the right food, *real food*, is not only going to affect your physical health but your mental well-being as well. It is all tied together. If you eat well, you will feel well. If you eat donuts, you will look like a donut. It's simple.

We used to treat the mind and body separately, mental and physical health as two completely different realms. However, we are learning more and more about brain health and how it is directly related to what we feed ourselves and how we treat our bodies.

To get the most out of both, you should be exercising regularly. Now, I understand this is not news that moving our bodies is going to help us with physical fitness. But it will also help us dramatically with our mental fitness.

What is it about motion, athletics, working out, yoga, or any form of physical activity that helps us feel better emotionally? And keep in mind, it doesn't have to be an hour sweating at the gym every single day; any form of motion is going to be beneficial.

JUST SQUAT.

IF YOU ARE IN A BAD HEADSPACE,
JUST SQUAT.

~

**DO THIS:** Have you done your squats yet? Start right now; write down how you feel then give me 25 squats, then write down how you feel afterward.

Then call a friend and tell them you are going to start walking/ exercising and eating better, make yourself accountable. Ask them if they want to join in and make a challenge with each other.

~

On a basic level, we are counting on the activity to boost our serotonin and dopamine levels. This is our best defense against depression, anxiety, and stress.

These are the "feel-good" neurotransmitters that occur naturally in our bodies. However, when we abuse ourselves with alcohol, drugs, sugar, and chemical-laden desserts, we can either increase the release of these or dramatically reduce them. I'll get more into this later.

You need to find an activity to plug into every single day. Walking, running, cycling, spin class, lifting weights, Jazzercise®, sex, anything. Even some simple squats, anywhere, anytime.

I'm not talking about training for a marathon or anything crazy like that. It is possible to exercise too much, causing damage to your body and heart.

I am merely advocating for a moderate level, which will get your heart pumping. Also, some sweating has been proven to be beneficial, so don't be afraid to sweat a little. And breathing hard is always a good thing.

If you don't physically feel good, you won't mentally feel right either.

Another critical component of mental and physical acuity is regular mindfulness or spiritual practice.

This can be combined with an activity like walking or cross-country skiing, which will help you clear your head while participating. Or, it can be a focused meditation practice with or without a spiritual component.

And spirituality does not have to be religious. I think of it as plugging into something you enjoy, something which feels good and that you appreciate as being more significant than just yourself.

Some call it a "Higher Power," but I call it "Universe." If you don't stay positive and grounded, you will never get the things you want or desire. You also need to connect with the universal energy which is available to you, even if you have learned it is not.

When you practice a consistent mindfulness and spirituality exercise, combined with a focus on body health and wellness, you will see results.

~

**DO THIS:** Download a meditation app like Calm, Waking Up, or Headspace. Take the time to start using it every single day. Every day, even if it is just for five minutes. Did I mention I want you to use it every day?

~

I'm telling you right now that you need to eat well, move your body, and "plug into" something every day if you expect to achieve success on any level. And you need to do this first before you can begin to realize any benefit from any of the other Principles I am going to share in this book.

I know what you're thinking right now.

"I can't afford to eat organic, real food all the time."

Discount organic food stores like Aldi are now becoming more common.

"I don't have the time to go for a walk or meditate. I'm too busy."

You can do squats while you are on the phone at work or when you are at home doing the dishes.

You must make health and fitness, both mentally and physically, your number one priority. Or you can put this book down right now and go on living the way you are living, and not much will change.

This is the foundation upon which all the other Principles sit, and I'm going to give you some simple, yet practical steps to get started.

Your body, mind, and spirit have to be clear and aligned to attract positive energy. Remember, energy is flowing. It moves through you. If you are not feeling well, first, you will be distracted by that issue, and second, the energy won't flow.

Think about the last time you overate at Thanksgiving dinner; how did you feel? You were stuffed probably, sleepy, and lounged around. Your brain was happy but not ready to work or create and manifest because your body was overly fed and full of carbs. Your biggest thought was a nap.

So here is what you need to do to get moving. Clear your mind, your body, and your spirit so the energy can move.

It does not have to be expensive or complicated. Anyone can do this, on any budget.

First, put down the donut. Or Pop-Tart®, energy drink, the bag of Cheetos, candy bar, or whatever bit of processed, fake food you are putting into your body and your brain.

I get it, and this is probably the hardest part. I didn't say it was easy. I said it was simple.

This was my most significant life challenge. I was a sugar junkie to the core. And it took a new dedication, maybe a bit of a new addiction, to a yoga mat to set me free.

At one point, I was on the floor eating a cake with my hands, trying to make myself feel better, not knowing which direction I wanted to go in my life. And at that time, the cake made me feel safe, secure, and happy...for a short window of time.

It filled my emptiness inside, but it certainly didn't fuel me physically, mentally, or spiritually.

I only thought it did.

When I learned to trade the cake for a yoga mat and use exercise to boost my serotonin and dopamine levels instead of external sources, I finally discovered and began to understand true happiness.

I understand there will be cravings and triggers, times when you can't say, "No." To help with all of that and to boost your serotonin levels, I want you to replace your sugary, carb-loaded desserts with real food snacks and meals.

Reaching for ice cream every evening or an alcoholic drink after work every night is a habit that can be replaced with a new, better pattern. New habits can be formed in 21 days. If you do the same thing for 21 days, you have a good chance of developing a new practice.

Instead of cookies, eat a piece of real turkey, not lunch meat, and some sweet potato. The tryptophan in these will boost your serotonin and dopamine, reducing your cravings for sugar or other substances. Save the alcohol for special occasions, or try quitting altogether for a chunk of time, and swap that beer or wine with a protein smoothie or a glass of water.

Without getting too technical, the protein is going to boost your serotonin and level out your blood sugar. Your cravings will be reduced, your brain will function better, and you will start making better choices.

Be sure to eat real, whole foods, things without a list of ingredients. Eat organic if you can, and you will find yourself eating less quantity and higher quality. Most people can afford to eat real food when they cut out all the desserts, high-priced energy or coffee drinks, and empty calories.

However, I understand it can be hard to break all of your bad habits at once, and everybody has a vice, usually for a reason. I tend to gravitate towards highly caffeinated drinks. After going to a naturopath, I discovered my adrenals were not correctly processing foods. I got on a digestive enzyme which has relaxed my adrenal system and allowed it to do its work.

That is all to start. You don't have to count calories or weigh your food. If you eliminate all processed food and sugar, you are doing better than 99% of everyone else and are well on your way.

Next up, drink plenty of water. Good, clean water, and lots of it. Almost all of us go around dehydrated all day every day, and it's making us sluggish, irritable, and keeps our brains from working efficiently. You can not create if you cannot think clearly, and water is usually the easiest fix.

All those chemical reactions work best if there is plenty of water, so get some. For every glass of caffeinated beverage you drink, you will need two glasses of water to zero it out. And on top of that, you should be gulping about eight glasses of water each day.

Then I want you to do some squats. Anytime you want to reach for sugar or feel stressed. When you need a break from work or are feeling depressed, I want you to put your hands behind your head, straighten your back, put your feet slightly spread apart, breathe deeply, and do 25 squats.

You can do these anywhere, anytime. It doesn't cost anything, and your hands aren't going to get dirty. But it will get your heart pumping, oxygen flowing, and boost your serotonin levels. You will feel better, and your cravings will be reduced while your brain fog clears.

And hey, if you have the time and inclination, by all means, go for a brisk walk, trail run, bicycle ride, swim, or hit the gym.

Again, the easiest way to begin to incorporate this healthy habit is to replace something you are already doing, combine it with something else, or reward yourself.

For example, let's say you love to watch Netflix®, I mean, who doesn't? But before you start that binge session, why not go for your walk and reward yourself with the TV. Or only watch your show on certain evenings and go for that walk on the other evenings. Or do your squats in front of your TV, I can frequently be seen doing squats in front of Charlie Sheen on *Two and a Half Men*, almost every night.

I even heard a story about someone who had rigged up his exercise bike to his Netflix® account. When he logged in, his show would play if he was pedaling a certain speed. If he slowed down or stopped, the show would pause.

That's a little extreme, but I think you get my point. Make some form of movement your priority every day, not relaxing, and you will begin to feel a difference.

Next, I want you to meditate if you aren't already. This isn't about sitting in a lotus position and chanting, completely shutting down your mind.

This is about calming your thoughts, breathing deeply, sitting comfortably, or even combining your "meditation" with a walk or yoga practice.

If you have a smartphone, and I know you do, there are plenty of meditation apps available that will guide you through the process. I use the Calm app, and I regularly use it to quiet my mind, even if it's just a 15-second session.

Sometimes people have trouble relaxing their brain, especially if they are Type A, and feel that meditation is too "granola" or "frou-frou." I have discovered a "Fuck That" mediation, which helps some people who find the curse words used in the guided meditation to be calming. It works for me when I'm amped up, to listen to it for the minute or two it plays, and I can relax.

Think about how you can make this a part of your daily routine. Find a way to create, replace, or add to an existing habit.

I have a friend who meditates every morning for about five minutes, that's it, and it does wonders for him. He gets up and heats his water for his coffee, which he makes in a press-pot. He puts the kettle on the burner, and while waiting for it to boil, he sits in a very comfortable chair, breathing deeply and relaxing, eyes closed.

By the time the kettle starts to whistle, he has his mind ready to start his day and plenty of oxygen in his system. By using the pot as a timer, it is never the same length of time because the amount of water varies slightly.

And he does all of this before he ever checks his phone or gets his brain filled with "to-do's" and tasks and the busyness of life.

His habit of drinking coffee is paired with meditation. They happen together, and both help him start a productive day.

Finally, I want to build on your fitness focus because it will help reduce anxiety.

We live in an increasingly anxious world, the mental and physical stimuli we are subjected to every day can get our brains stuck in a fight or flight mode, always stressed. This floods our bodies with cortisol, and it also prevents us from getting into a creative state of being. You end up reactive all the time instead of proactive.

This, in turn, makes it extremely difficult to maintain a positive mindset, and if you can't be positive, if you are always negative, you will never achieve the things you want to happen.

To reduce your anxiety, in addition to the physical and mental fitness things I've already outlined, I want you to breathe.

In general, people don't breathe very well, and it is something we don't practice. You must stand up tall, put your shoulders back, ground your feet, and take deep breaths. You can use a yoga breathing technique, I often recommend. It's three counts while breathing in, and three counts breathing out. Three in, three out.

Breathing like this will instantly ground you to the earth and help you to relax.

Set the alarm on your phone or pair it with another activity to remind yourself to take a moment and breathe, breathe deeply, and fill your body with fresh oxygen.

You can't create if you aren't relaxed and if you are in constant worry or stress mode. Breathe, get grounded, think positively.

Another thing I want you to do to keep anxiety at bay is to take a bath. And breathe while you are soaking in the tub, do some meditation maybe. Put on some soft music, throw in a bath bomb or Epsom salts, a few drops of lavender oil, turn down the lights, and get some candles.

Relax and shut off the brain for a while. It is a necessary activity to create and flow with the Law of Attraction.

~

**DO THIS:** When you are shopping, be sure and pick up some Epsom salts or bath bombs. You can also throw in some lavender essential oil and baking soda for a super detox bath, which I recommend once each week.

Use them tonight along with your diffuser. No diffuser? You can pick one up inexpensively or merely make a cup of mint tea. Breathe in the aroma deeply.

~

Our parents knew this trick, how many times did they toss you in the tub before bedtime to help calm you down and shift your focus from playtime and excitement to bedtime and calmness.

And if you are a parent, you know what I'm talking about. And it's not just the physical relaxation of the warm water, but the mind is shifting from your busy day to a new, more peaceful energy.

Now the final suggestions I have to help you achieve optimum energy levels are all about getting some good, restful sleep.

I want you to try this every night when you go to bed, leave your phone in another room. No screens in your bedroom allowed. No TV, no laptop, no phone.

Replace your nightly social media session while lying in bed with a journaling session. When going to bed, write down anything and everything. Just write and get all the garbage out of your head, even if it is only for a few minutes.

Be sure and give yourself enough time for adequate sleep. Seven hours at a minimum will keep your body and brain out of fight or flight mode.

You can also sleep with a diffuser, and lavender will again do the trick to help you relax. And pull down the shades, make it dark and quiet, a cozy cave.

I know this all sounds like a lot and that you might be feeling a little overwhelmed by this sudden change in your world.

New food, new exercise routines, remembering to breathe and do squats, journaling, sleeping, meditating, and taking candle baths.

You don't have to make all these changes all at once, but you need to start now, even if it's with some deep breathing.

~

**DO THIS:** Did I say to breathe? I think I did. I want you to breathe, and not as you have been, but deeply and with intention.

Use the 3-count breathing technique and stand up straight. Dig your heels into the ground and imagine a pole running the length of your body from your forehead, along your spine, and into the ground.

Set the alarm on your phone to remind yourself to take a "breath break" every couple of hours.

~

I'll have a checklist for you, but I highly recommend setting up reminders with your phone or putting sticky notes on your bathroom mirror to remind you to do some squats or to breathe deeply. Because if you don't find a way to detoxify your body and mind, your success goals are just dreams and wishes, they will not become a reality no matter how positive your attitude is.

Your attitude starts in your body, and this is connected to your mind.

Bad habits are hard to break, and so are good ones. I want you to focus on creating useful, healthy habits, and the bad ones will fall away because they will be replaced.

For almost everyone, brushing their teeth at least twice a day is something they will not miss and will feel wrong about if they do. Why? Four-year-olds scream about brushing their teeth and would gladly never do it unless their parents remind them over and over to brush their teeth.

It's become such an ingrained habit that it feels good. You can do this too with the new, simple activities I've mentioned here.

That's how it was with yoga for me. Before yoga, I just wanted to shove a whole cake in my mouth; that is what felt right. At least temporarily, because overeating sugar leaves anyone feeling like shit.

I replaced my sugar habit with a yoga habit, and I'll be honest, at first yoga sucked. It was painful. I was not flexible. I could hardly breathe at times and was shaky all over.

But over time, it got better. I gained flexibility, it hurt less, but I somehow managed to like the pain, or the release of the pain after coming out of a pose. I could breathe deeply, I quit shaking, and it feels good. Damn good. It is something that I need in my life now because if I miss it for too long, it's as if I haven't brushed my teeth, I feel yucky.

~

*Rebecca called and said, "I think I want to divorce my husband because every day at 4:00 when I leave work, I'm depressed and don't want to come home."*

*I said, "Okay, no divorce just yet. Let's keep a food-mood journal so that I can see throughout the day what you eat and how you feel."*

*Her reaction, "This is stupid! I'm paying for this?"*

*And I said, "Yes because your food and your mood are tied, I want to rule out crappy food. I want to make sure you really are depressed going home."*

*And of course, she asked, "Well, can't you just give me medication for depression?"*

*"No, let's see what you're eating first."*

*Her food-mood journal came back after seven days. Breakfast was egg white omelets with coffee, no sugar. And then around 9:00, she had some nuts and some dried fruit. For lunch, she had a grilled chicken salad and a little tiny roll with a little bit of butter.*

*But every day at 2:00 pm she had two Boston cream donuts. Everyday.*

*She worked at the firehouse, and the fire guys would bring in these donuts.*

*I said to her, "You're not depressed. Your sugar and your insulin have plummeted because between two and four you are eating over 100 grams of sugar and fat, and the bottom dropped out. It's sugar, and you're crashing."*

*"It can't be that easy," she says.*

*And I said, "It is that easy. Let's take the donuts out, replace them with a protein shake, or something high in protein like natural peanut butter with some apples."*

*She did. And on Day One, she called me and reported that she didn't feel any different.*

*I said, "Well, you have to take some time to detox from it. You will have some emotional issues tied to it."*

*Day Two, she called, "I feel cranky between 2:00 and 4:00 and feel like I'm denied my donut."*

*I told her to eat a banana, some dried fruit, and some nuts for a snack to help level out her blood sugar and give her enough energy to make it through the day.*

*By Day Four, she reported, "I don't feel depressed. I feel better, and I think I'm okay."*

*By Day Five, she had no depression, and at 4:00 pm she was excited to go home. She had come to realize her irritability was directly tied to her food and eating habits, and that better blood sugar management could save her marriage.*

~

**DO THIS:** Start a journal to help purge your junk from your mind every night. This is just free-form writing, write whatever you want, get it out.

Put it by your bed instead of your phone and write in it every night. Every single night. Which nights? Yes, every night, you got it. Or, you can also do it in the morning, but do it.

~

Sometimes we misconstrue a feeling or emotion or anxiety, which is directly tied to food because our food mood is tied together, and we project it onto someone else. We may be cranky and assume it's because of our husband or someone else in our lives when it's just a food-related issue where our blood sugar and body chemistry is off. If you can find a way to straighten out your chemistry, your mood will also adjust, and you'll be less likely to argue or become angry.

You have heard the term "Hangry," where you get angry because you are hungry. Make sure you are not hungry!

Rebecca now had real food on board, supporting her natural serotonin and dopamine instead of the chemical-laden donuts.

It can be something as simple as keeping a food-mood journal and looking at your diet, which can dictate your moods. If you're not feeling good, you're not going to work out. You're going to eat more garbage and sit on the sofa and binge-watch Netflix®.

Swap your habits like Rebecca did. When she changed her routine of eating the donuts for eating a banana and some nuts, she quickly started to feel the results.

You will feel them too.

~

**DO THIS:** Go to our site at www.UnpauseYourLife.com and tell us how you are doing? I want to see before and after pictures of your fridge and pantry.

# CHAPTER TWO

# CREATING MY SELF AND DISCOVERING MY PURPOSE IN LIFE

## *Who Am I and What Should I Be Doing?*

Most people have an authentic self, and then there is a separate view of who they're supposed to be. It's almost like two completely different personas.

First, you have the persona that you're told to be, that society or your family says, " This is the role you take." For example, a woman. A woman is supposed to bear children because that's the message she hears from society or her family. That's her function, and it's something that she can do that men cannot, this separates her and sets her apart.

When a woman says, "I'm not going to have kids," it goes against society's expected persona of a woman.

Her authentic self says, "I don't want children," but society would condemn her and say, "You have to have kids," or "You're supposed to have kids. This is what you do. You have a gift of a uterus, so that's your job. That's your function."

People who go against the grain or go against society or their family's expectations might not know it, but they are following their authentic selves.

Now, people have trouble figuring out their authentic selves because they have these things that go against their true nature. I was told growing up that I should do all kinds of things that were entirely not me. I grew up in an Italian and Slovak family, and that I was taught that would grow up and marry a local boy, get a job at the mall, move two doors down and pop out kids. I ultimately went against their wishes and even became the first one to go to college in my family.

My dad, grandmother, and stepfather never graduated high school.

When I told them I was going to college, their response was, "Why? You don't go to college in our family."

And I said, "That's not in alignment with my authentic self. It's not who I am."

My mother's dream for me was to get a job at the mall and eventually move into a managerial position. She wanted me to get a house, live close by, and have grandbabies for her to cuddle and play with.

I packed my stuff up and bolted. I couldn't handle what my family's goals for me were, to me, they had set the bar too low. I don't think popping out kids, not going to college, not making something of your life is any good. And getting divorced in your 40s after you realized you hate your spouse, you haven't explored life, and you're having a mid-life crisis because you never lived an authentic life is something I had no interest in.

I lost touch with my family for years because I did not follow their path and my choices were not accepted. I was not going to be happy being the "under-achiever" they wanted me to be.

On the flip side, what happens to many people is the complete opposite. They are pushed to become accountants, doctors, lawyers to appease their Mom and Dad or conform to society's expectations. They end up in a job or career they can't stand because it goes against their authentic selves.

Unfortunately, this can often lead to substance abuse to cope.

My husband was on the "outs" with his dad for almost sixteen years.

His parents were expecting him to be an "overa-chiever" like the rest of the family. He grew up, and his Mom and Dad told him, "You're going to go to college."

But his reply? "I don't want to go to college. I want to be a musician."

And his Dad insists, "Well, I went to college, and now I'm a superintendent. Mom's a school teacher. We all went to college. We have our Master's degrees."

Both his brothers did as told and got degrees. Now, his older brother works for NASA, and he builds spaceships. His younger brother went to college too. He has almost his Ph.D., and he's the head psycholo-gist for Orlando School System.

"So, you're going to go to college."

And in this instance, my husband said, "I want to be a drummer in a rock band."

Even though he had a full scholarship waiting for him (he was a kickass baseball player), he left home. His authentic self desired to be an entertainer, but his persona or the person that he was expected to be by his family's standards: to be an athlete, get an excellent job, marry a nice girl, start a beautiful family, did not resonate with his authentic self. He went against everything, and everyone, to be his authentic self.

His family was the opposite of mine, and they told him that he had to go to college to support a family and to get a good job.

We both had to go against the expectations of our loved ones to find and live our true purpose.

Most people struggle for years because they are prisoners and cannot be themselves. Sometimes the family will cut them off financially, cut them out of the will or inheritance, or simply not visit or call often.

In my case, no one would visit, I had to go home, and no one wanted to discuss my success or endeavors. Most family members had no idea what I even did. Life was not always easy because I had no financial or emotional family support, but I knew deep down it was what I needed to do to get the most out of my life.

~

*I always have a "Bucket List" going, 25 things I want to do before I die. And why is that important? It's because you still must be working toward your goals and I also feel it has to be fun. Life must be fun at some point.*

*When I was fourteen, we were sitting at the dinner table. It was a Friday night, which was "take out night." We never went out to eat because we didn't have the money, but on Friday we would get pizza or a big bucket of KFC chicken.*

*My stepdad was a welder and a truck driver, and he had holes in his shirt, my mom was still in her scrubs from her job as a file clerk at the local hospital. They both look exhausted. Dinner conversations were not of fancy trips or family vacations.*

*We had two piece-of-shit used cars, and we're barely making any money. We live in my grandmother's house. Every trip I wanted to go on in high school or event I wanted to attend, I was not able to because as my mom put it, 'there is no money for that.'*

*So Friday night dinner was the highlight. And maybe a game of cards after.*

*My stepdad asks me, "So what's your plan?"*

*I'll never forget it. I said, "Well, I have four goals."*

*"What are they?"*

I replied, "I want to make a million dollars."

He laughed. He says, "Okay. We don't come from money, and we're middle class. You'll never make a million dollars."

"Number two; I want to have a new car. I want to walk in and buy a car off the showroom floor."

"Next," I said, "I want a house by the beach—because we're two and a half hours from the beach."

Then I finished with, "And I also want to find a real man because I'm not going to find one around here."

That made him laugh even more.

So, we had a running joke that every holiday I would get one of those four things.

One year he made me a shadow box that was my house by the beach. He did the whole thing. It was cool, and I still have it.

One year he found this toy jeep, and he mounted it and did all this cool stuff with it. It was my ideal tricked out car.

He bought me a "million-dollar" towel for a blanket. I still have it.

And for the real man, he gave me a Dildo. And I'll never forget how horrified my grandmother was at Christmas when I opened it.

*He explained, "You can attain the first three, but you sure as hell can't attain that last one, so this is the second-best."*

*He encouraged me. Whereas my father said, "You can't do anything. You'll never attain any goals."*

*My authentic self said, "Yes, I will."*

*And my bucket list was there at 14.*

*By the time I was 33 I had obtained all but one. And then I lost three, but I was able to get all again and even the last one, the "Real Man," when I started over.*

*I hit my Bucket List.*

*I made $4.1 million when I was 32. I bought a brand-new Dodge SRT8 Charger, candy-apple red, the day it came out onto the floor, with cash, and I had a house on the beach in Galveston, Texas. And the man, well I got my man.*

~

While I was out living my authentic self, so was my future husband, but at a price.

He felt guilty for leaving his family and moving from Florida to California to live his dream. He eventually returned to start a family and the stress for him of the 'normal' 9-5 was too much, My future husband eventually turned to drugs and alcohol to deal with the stress and anxiety he felt while trying to live a self that was not his own; one he was told he should be living.

I, on the other hand, pretty much said, "F- you, I'm going to do what I want, get outta my way. I'm not going to get suckered into having kids."

And I did, to this day I have none (well stepkids and those that hang out and eat my food).

Different personas will handle various situations in unique ways. My family didn't want me to get any higher education, and they complained they didn't even know how to help me fill out a college entrance application. This attitude alone almost made me work that much harder to get it done myself. It's hard to say precisely, but my experience and reaction would have been a world of difference if I was wearing my husband's shoes, having a family who actively encouraged me to go to college.

We both had to go against the grain in our way to get to our authentic selves. He had everything handed to him, and I can count on one hand the number of gifts my father gave me. I had to earn my way the hard way to get what I wanted or needed.

And when my husband didn't go off to college, he was no longer supported, he got nothing. But, I never had much, so I always had to figure out who I was, where I was going, how to get what I wanted, but he didn't, it was all provided.

Creating your authentic self is very difficult because families and societies expect that they know who we should be when we know deep inside. We are not that person. We're someone else. Does that make sense?

When I tell people about this, their initial response often is, "Wow, I get it. I can see how that can happen to a lot of people, even myself. How you can get trapped into becoming someone you aren't."

Next, they ask, "What should I do to create my authentic self? What should I do first?"

~

 **DO THIS**: Make a list of things you Love, Dislike, and Will Tolerate. Three columns. Then list everything you can think of from food, to work, to behaviors, to the fun. Figuring out who you are and where you are headed starts with what you like, don't like, and what you will tolerate.

~

For me, working for someone else is on the "can't stand" list. I am an entrepreneur, and I won't be able to work for anyone but me. Also, for me, scuba diving is on the "can't stand" list. I'm never going to scuba dive, and I'm okay with that.

The second thing you do is answer these questions: What gives me energy or joy or excitement? What fulfills me and "fills my cup?"

If you think of a cup that you are pouring into and when it is full, you feel good. Whatever makes you want to jump out of bed, ready to start the day, excited for life.

And you take your "like" list, and you look at it, and you say, "What do I get enjoyment out of?"

Sure, you might like playing with the puppy, but it also comes with walking the puppy, and feeding the puppy, and bathing the puppy, and cleaning up after the puppy. If you don't like all those things, you really shouldn't be a dog owner. Does the puppy bring you joy? If the puppy brings you joy, then those mundane activities, like walking the dog and cleaning up and all that will be not an issue because you have so much pleasure from the puppy.

But we want to know what brings you joy and happiness.

Next, we're going to think not only about the question "What do I like?" but "What is my passion in life? What is my purpose?"

You must figure out what your passions are to understand your purpose. Because if you're passionate about creating artwork, your goal may be an artist, but your purpose also may be a museum curator.

What makes you get out of bed in the morning and brings you joy? Why do you wake up in the morning?

And that's the problem where people sometimes get stuck. If they get up and they say, "Crap, I got to go to work. I'm going to be there all day. Is it the weekend yet?"

And they're looking at the clock. It's two o'clock. "It's *only* two o'clock." And people will eat poorly, or take a cigarette break, or play video games, or surf their social media accounts to get through their day,

"I want to get through the day, and that's my reward to deal with this stupid job."

Well, if the day is going too slow and you're just going through the motions of life, you're not living your authentic self. There's no way you're happy. You might be temporarily happy eating the donut or playing the video game because it boosts your serotonin in your brain and your dopamine, but you're not thrilled about going to work. It is just a distraction.

You've got to figure out what your passion is and *create your reality.*

To do that, we figure out what your skill sets are, your knowledge base, and your motivation. And to figure out those three things, we write.

You make a list. What am I good at doing? What is my knowledge base, and what is my motivation? Because you could be the smartest person on the planet, but if you are not motivated, you're not going to do squat. You must get motivated to make your goal happen.

Where people get stuck creating their authentic self is thinking, "This is a lot of work." Yes, it is. Starting with the basis of just figuring out "who I am" and "what I like" is ground zero.

I also use this approach when people ask, "Well, how do I attract my perfect mate?"

You must know who you are first. That's why people half the time say, "I'm with the wrong person. I keep seeking the wrong man. I keep seeking the wrong woman. I don't understand."

Because they have no idea who they are. If you don't know who you are, you're not going to see what you want. If you don't know what you want, you're going to attract everything you don't want because you're focusing on the negative.

All of this can be very hard for people. They don't know who they are, and it's easy to then go through the motions because this is what's told to them, and they have pressure. The pressure of mom and dad who are saying, "You're twenty-five, you should have a job," or "You are 35, why are you not married?"

~

**DO THIS**: List 25 adjectives to describe yourself.

Okay, look at your list. Did you write, "I'm a Mom" or "I'm a teacher?" That's not who you are; that's what you do, that's your job function.

~

In my case, I was 34, I had created a multi-million-dollar company in the fitness industry, at the top of my game, and my mother quizzed me, "Are you a lesbian? Because you have not married. Where are my grandbabies?"

I was career-focused, not desiring a family, and said, "I don't need a husband. I'm perfectly fine, making right with the dollars, doing my thing. I'll take a husband when I'm ready."

And that was a battle because in my family you get married at twenty-three, you make babies, and by the time you're forty, forty-five, your kids have grown.

Why would I want to do that? I had no interest in following that path, and that's my authentic self. I was more interested in creating my plan, my own life.

Finally, I got married, and I married someone they did not expect.

When I became engaged, my mother asked me if he was a lawyer or a doctor or some other professional. When I told her that he was a drummer in a rock band, she replied, "Oh honey, you're going to work for the rest of your life, musicians don't make any money."

What my family did is take the family's self-identity, the family's authenticity, and provide an expectation that I continue the family traditions. My grandmother has two daughters, and her daughter (my mother) has two daughters, and my sister has two daughters. The expectation was I would also provide children.

"This is what we do."

Every woman in my family, my mother, my sister, my grandmother, her mother, her grandmother, all were caretakers. They all worked in health care, from the hospital setting to chiropractic. I can't stand the hospital. I hate it. Blood, disease, death, and dying, no thank you. I have no interest in that. And the smell of hospital to me is horrible, it's like a hospice. I am an empath, I pick up people's energies, and a hospital is a trauma. No thank you, that is not in alignment with my higher self.

~

*When I was fifteen, I was told to be a candy striper. And I did the candy striper thing at the hospital.*

*I lasted two days, I vomited, and that was the end of it.*

*And my grandmother asked me, "What are you going to do? Because this is what we do, we work at the hospital."*

*"I'm not working at the hospital," I informed her.*

*She said, "Well, I don't know what to tell you."*

*And there was no other advice.*

*When I said I wanted to go to college, my mother was stumped, "Well, I don't know what to do with that. I don't know what to tell you."*

*I was left alone at eighteen to figure out how to fill out these complicated application forms.*

*I learned early on that my authentic self meant that I must be a warrior. I must be a trailblazer. I must do these things on my own because I have no support and to be okay with that because that's part of my authentic self.*

~

I am in an industry where I help people, but I also give them a reality check of what's happening, not just taking care of their physical health. I can handle that. I can take someone from the darkest of days and demons and get them to the other side to love their life and be ready to take over the world.

And I work from home with a laptop and a phone.

And I love it.

And I travel all over the world for my clients.

And I love it.

And I sometimes spend only three days a month in own my bed.

And I love every minute of it.

I could never go to the hospital to work a 9-5. That is like a prison to me.

Now, I know most people are afraid to fail, and so they'll listen to their family or whoever else is giving them the advice, especially if there is someone else paying for their education or supporting them. Once money is involved, it does change the game, and a lot of people will go to college or trade school even if they don't want to, the pressure is on because of the financial situation.

They can justify their decisions, "Well, they told me I should do this. I guess I should."

For example, I want nothing to do with real estate, but my father is a broker, and he offered to pay for my real estate training courses if I went. I went and then sold one house, and I quit. He expected me to take over his company, and it did not interest me at all.

Following friends is another life trap. "This is what my friend did. It worked for her," or "All my friends are getting married." There is also a lot of power in FOMO, or Fear Of Missing Out.

I hear that "All my friends were getting married. I guess I should." "All my friends have kids. I guess I should." "All my friends are getting divorced. I guess I should."

It's a path that many get caught up with because of age and expectations. When people finish high school, it's time to go to college. Then it's time to get married and have children. And if we aren't on that path, we can often feel like there is something wrong with us, and we are missing out on these crucial once-in-a-lifetime events.

I hear people say how important it is to have kids and that they can "change your life." Well, I'm here to tell you, launching and running a successful business will change your life too. Yes, both will sometimes require you to stay up late, work extra hard, and clean up messes. And they both have different rewards and the fear of missing out on one thing, say having children, will often require you to sacrifice something else, like starting a business.

People go through the motions. And you see the women that are lost at forty-five, there's a ton of my friends that are forty-five and single.

And they say, "How did I get here? How did this happen? Twenty years ago, I was hot and fun and had the world in front of me, and here I am, and the best thing I have to show for it all is two kids and an ex-husband."

They thought that's what they needed to do to make their life full or be happy, right? I mean, people get stuck into chasing the next thing.

"What's going to make me happy right now?"

And we never stop and think, "If this makes me happy right now, will this make me happy in five years, ten years, fifteen years? Is this going to make me happy long-term?"

If they knew that, they would've had the fast cars all along, ever since they were 22.

Right about now, this is when we start to see the "mid-life crisis" starting to pop up. The guys are getting the fast cars, the women getting boob jobs. These people never figured out who they are, and they are still trying. They are trying to bring back their youth and fun, and maybe they are afraid to age, especially because now they're getting old, and still don't know who their authentic self is or what they want.

When it comes to making money, you look at what's going to make me money now, what's going to make me money in a year and what's going to make me money long-term.

Your life is no different. Because if you say right now, "I want a baby because all my friends have babies and baby showers," and you have a kid, three years from now you're not going to have the same feeling you had three years prior.

People have to sit down and plan, "Where do I want to be in one year? Five years, ten years, tomorrow?"

And not go with what they're told to go with but what they want to do and where they see themselves going. And that goes back to your authentic self, which goes back to your moral compass because everybody has a moral compass.

They know right from wrong based upon the compass they received from their family. You use this compass early on, to create who you are because you know right from wrong.

My grandmother said to me, "You will never lie, and you will never cheat, and you will never steal."

I take a penny from the bank, and I feel guilty. Why? Because my grandmother instilled in me that the moral compass is if you steal something, it's terrible.

Now, she's very religious, threatening with God and Jesus and making me feel guilty.

One day I walked out of my gym, and there was a towel around my neck, and I went right back up, and I said, "Wow, you guys didn't even stop me. I stole a towel."

I feel horrible. But that's my moral compass. What happens is people don't know their moral compass, and sometimes they use their moral compass to their advantage.

For example, even though someone doesn't lie, cheat, or steal, they might tell a white lie because it gets them what they need right now. These "opportunists" will take every advantage and angle to get what they want, even if it's morally wrong. They do know who they are but don't like who they are. And they prey on people who don't know themselves and aren't strong enough to say, "That's not going to happen."

When they diverted their moral compass for that white lie, they are in their authentic self because their authentic self is a liar, and if that's true, they don't want to look at that. That's why they don't want to see their authentic selves. I call this a circle problem.

They will tell lies so often you will believe they aren't lying, and eventually, they convince themselves the lies aren't a problem.

The vast majority of us have a decent moral compass, and when we wake up in the morning, we don't think, "I want to be a money-launderer." We may be thinking that we want to get rich, and somewhere along the line, the "opportunist" sees a way to make a lot of money that may not be legal. Next thing you know, they're a criminal, even though that's not what they set out to do.

The "opportunist" latched onto this without referring to or following their moral compass as an easy way to get to their ultimate goal, being rich. It's not that they wanted to be a criminal and end up in jail, but they didn't figure out a better way to make money, they haven't created a way to get to their goal.

So, we've talked a lot about finding or creating our authentic self, and now I want to go a little deeper into discovering your purpose.

For me, when I first started, I wanted to be an FBI agent. That sounded awesome to me, felt great, like it would a lot of fun. It got me started on my path, and I never did become an agent, but it helped lead me to where I am today.

The other thing I felt when I was thinking about working for the FBI was excitement. I would get an instant adrenaline boost just thinking about it, have you ever experienced that?

That excitement is going to give you energy, the energy you are going to need to keep you motivated and moving towards your intended target when times get tough, the shit hits the fan, and you feel like throwing in the towel because that will happen.

There is a pattern when you decide on a new adventure. First, you're all fired up, excited, and full of enthusiasm. Then, as you get into it more, and learn more about whatever it is, the excitement wears off. Maybe you get bored, or the end goal starts to seem too far away, or it becomes a bit tedious.

During this period of disinterest, you can easily be distracted, like a dog noticing a squirrel. And off you go chasing the next exciting thing. Something is happening here, which allows you to lose focus. Either you genuinely don't want to do this, or you haven't stuck it out long enough.

When your new venture starts to become not so unique anymore, and your enthusiasm breaks down, you may have to dig deep to pull up those first feelings, the energy you felt when you initially set out on that particular journey.

Sometimes people don't research what they're supposed to be doing, and they don't study the time that takes to get there or what happens when they get there. They're always just in the moment. While we're discovering what we want to do, we also have to look at the downtime, the uptime, and the financial side of it.

When you're discovering what you want to do, is it financially enough? What location in the world is it? Do you want to be there? How long is it going to take for you to get where you want to go? And once you're there, are you going to be bored? These are things we have to consider.

Of course, another area you need to take into consideration when deciding upon a particular path or opportunity is your skillset. What are you good at doing? We all have a certain tendency to be drawn to specific tasks because we feel satisfaction performing them and enjoy them.

Some people like math. For me, that sounds like torture, to crunch numbers all day. No thanks. A lot of it has to do with exposure, what are you exposed to while growing up, or in school or at work. It also has to do with what naturally or innately draws or attracts you. We often gravitate towards those things which are comfortable or easy, and we are then more likely to explore those further.

~

**DO THIS**: Take the Myers-Briggs Personality Type assessment at www.UnPauseYourLife.com.

Upon completion of this free questionnaire, you will obtain your 4-letter type formula according to Carl Jung's and Isabel Briggs Myers' typology, along with the strengths of preferences and the description of your personality type.

This will help you understand the communication and learning styles of your type, along with discovering careers and occupations most suitable for your personality type.

Look at the career list associated with your personality type. What resonates with you?

~

The Myers-Briggs Personality Type Indicator is a self-report inventory designed to identify a person's personality type, strengths, and preferences. The questionnaire was developed by Isabel Myers and her mother Katharine Briggs based on their work with Carl Jung's theory of personality types.

Today, the MBTI inventory is one of the most widely used psychological instruments in the world.

Based on the answers to the questions on the inventory, people are identified as having one of 16 personality types. The goal of the MBTI is to allow respondents to explore further and understand their personalities, including their likes, dislikes, strengths, weaknesses, possible career preferences, and compatibility with other people.

No one personality type is "best" or "better" than any other one. It isn't a tool designed to look for dysfunction or abnormality. Instead, its goal is to help you learn more about yourself.

When I took the quiz, I was 17 or 18 years old. I knew I always wanted to study psychology, but because I wanted to understand why my family was so fucked up, I thought I'd end up taking those courses. And when I took the quiz, FBI agent came up, a private investigator came up, and a psychologist came up, and so did lawyer, and I'm good at all of them. I ended up combining my skills to work in addiction.

I have to be a Private Eye in addiction because you're always figuring out what the person's doing. Like an FBI agent, I'm reading body language, like a lawyer, I'm defending my clients when they do something, and I go to court with them. And of course, I have the psychology background to complete all of them.

That's part of life, though, the piece I call "Universe," which places us in certain places at certain times to experience things. It's up to us to embrace the things we are good at and tap into those skills to help us get where we want to go. In my case, I enjoyed all of the career options and being devoted to just one of them bored me. I was able to integrate all of them into one career and enjoy my day to day job functions.

Another way to get to the core of your authentic self is to figure out your positive qualities and your negative qualities. You do this on a job application and a first date. You might say, "I am not good at cooking, but I can sure bake the best cake for dessert."

If you are unsure of your positive qualities or your negative qualities, ask someone close, someone who isn't going to bullshit you and candy-coat their response so they don't hurt your feelings.

And deep down, you likely know what you are good at or what your good qualities are, don't you? And you probably know what you suck at if you're perfectly honest with yourself, right?

These can be all kinds of things, but all of what I have been talking about here is almost always something innate to you, something with which you have been born.

~

**DO THIS**: Make a Positive and Negatives List.

What are your 25 positive traits and 25 negative traits? Every day focus on your top 10 positives. Put them on your mirror. Take your negative qualities and make them positive.

Need help? Head to www.UnpauseYourLife.com and grab a FREE PDF exercise to get going!

Something negative, "I am fat." You're not fat. Fat is something you have. It's not something you can be, so you're not fat. Your body has fat.

If you don't like the amount of fat your body has, let's look at what you're eating and look at your exercise. If you're eating right and you're not exercising, guess what? Your body will have more fat than it would if you were eating correctly and exercising.

Take those negatives and work on making them a positive by adding an action step.

"I am Fat" becomes...

"I am thin" and add the action step...

"I am thin because I workout and do not eat fast food."

~

If you've completed the Myers-Briggs assessment, it becomes fairly obvious to us at some point whether we like things organized or if we like to be more spontaneous and fly by the seat of our pants. Did you find that you are outgoing and extroverted, or are you someone who gets more energy from being alone and quiet?

If you completed the positive versus negative list traits as well, compare the notes. What did you notice? Do you see a pattern?

The assessment and list will show you what you are good at and what you enjoy. My point is that you should be focusing on the stuff you are naturally good at, the things you enjoy, and where you get energy. This whole notion of "gut feelings" is true much of the time. You know when you are excited about something, and it's fun, then it does not seem like work. But what happens when it is something you can't stand, and you are only doing it because you must? You will drag your feet and procrastinate, you will do a half-assed job, you bitch and moan, you will avoid it, and it will suck the energy from you ten times as fast as when you are in the zone, doing something you love.

Unfortunately, most of our world is full of people who end up in some shitty job they cannot stand just because they need to make money, and it's the only way they have discovered (so far) how to accomplish that. Could you imagine spending your entire life doing a shitty job you hate only to retire and die two years later? That's what's happening in our society.

People spend their whole lives working. My grandfather and my grandmother could not wait to retire because they wanted to travel throughout the United States, and he died when he was 60, two years after he retired, and they never got to do that because she was retiring. So, they waited their whole life to do something they never got to do. I've lived my life backward. I've traveled and enjoyed things ever since I was a late teen on my own because I didn't want to be the person who got sick and said, "I wish I could've seen Europe. I wish I could have seen the Grand Canyon. I wish I could have gone to Alaska."

I go now. Why? I'm still able-bodied to go, and because when I get to the point where I can't go, I want to have those memories.

Working and waiting to do these things causes enormous problems in our world, and it often results in the very issues with substance abuse my clients end up dealing with, just because they are using drugs and alcohol to cope with their unhappiness. Also, people may use other types of coping mechanisms such as scrolling through Facebook, Amazon Prime shopping, porn, anything to distract from the fact they hate their life, which means they're not living with their authentic self.

If you set your intentions correctly and focus on those things you like and that bring joy into your world, it's possible to be happy with who you are and what you are doing.

As I mentioned earlier in this chapter, the single biggest obstacle I see that keeps people from following their hearts is a fear of failure.

Often this has been drilled into us since we were little, that if we get something wrong or if we make a mistake, we have failed.

Nothing could be further from the truth. Your goal should not be never to make a mistake or to avoid failure completely but to go ahead and fail; that's how we learn.

When you were a baby, just learning to walk, and you took those first three steps and tipped over, plopped onto your butt. Your Mom or Dad or whoever was there didn't say, "Oops, well, looks like she can't walk. That's too bad. I guess she'll have to crawl the rest of her life."

No, you got up, and maybe with some help, you tried again and again until you got it — the same thing when you learned to ride a bike. Plenty of scraped knees, but now you can't "unknow" how to ride a bike, right?

This failure avoidance is a built-in system, so I understand why it's hard to fight. We are instinctually conditioned to avoid pain, so why the hell would we voluntarily subject ourselves to this pain of failing?

Succeeding feels even better, especially after a few stinging knock-downs. I've been there plenty of times myself.

Now, believe it or not, the next biggest obstacle I see is a fear of success. Because once you succeed, people will expect you to achieve every time. And once you set that bar, you can't go under the bar. This means if you fall under the bar, then you feel guilt, shame, and remorse over why you couldn't continue to do that, to have that level of success. Suddenly it becomes easier to stay in complacency or mediocracy and keep a job where you serve burgers at the fast-food joint.

> *"Life isn't about finding yourself. Life is about creating yourself."*
>
> – *George Bernard Shaw*

Once you realize that perfection is not possible, ever, it relieves a lot of pressure. And that the only way to succeed is to get up time and time again after you fall, then you will welcome mistakes and treat them as learning opportunities.

The other common obstacle that tends to go hand-in-hand with the fear of failure is the shame. Shame usually starts in childhood, and we will spend more time delving into this preconceived notion later in the book. Most people believe that failure is something to be embarrassed about or to sweep under the rug. But isn't there something about owning our failures that gives us the keys to success?

Be proud of your mistakes, be willing to admit them, and use them as fuel to feed the fires that stoke your determination to succeed. Mistakes make the man, and mistakes make who you are. The more errors you have, the more you learn, the more you learn, the more guidance you have, the more direction you have, the easier it is to create who you are.

Also, I want to say here, going back to our personality types a little, that it is okay to not be good at something. We all suck at something but don't let this get you down or prevent you from dialing in those things you are good at and can leverage as assets in your life.

Be okay with your "faults" because those are some of the things that make you who you are and help to make you unique. It would be a boring world if we were all good at everything. Different personality types are why we have different people for different jobs. I feel as a business owner, it's essential to hire people who are better than you are for specific tasks or duties.

For example, I hate to clean. I don't like to clean at all. I'm not good at it. It'll take me five to eight hours to clean a 900 square foot condo that would take a professional cleaner an hour and a half to do. It makes more sense for me to invest my time in working with clients than wasting five hours cleaning. It's easier for me to pay for the cleaner who does a better job in less time and I can focus on my area of genius, on the things I am good at and like to do.

The same thing with cooking, I don't like to cook. It takes me hours to cook and hours to clean the pans. That's why there are cooking services, people that show up with food that is prepared and ready to go. That is why there are restaurants. It's vital for you to delegate the work to people that are better than you in that area. You're not going to be skilled in every task, but you're going to be able to delegate.

You can delegate, you can be good at something. Whatever you learn, take it, harness it, and learn it as much as possible. So you become the expert in that thing. And it can be anything. If you're going to be the janitor, be the best janitor you can be.

> *"Treat the janitor and the CEO with the same respect."*

I mentioned it before, but your path, even if you know it's headed in the right direction, is not always going to be smooth sailing. Sometimes you will find yourself having to do a job you don't like, or are no good at, to get to the other side. It's important to keep your eye on the prize during these times and keep doing "it" even if you don't like it. If you have a strategy and plan to make sure you are moving through the discomfort and towards a better place on your path, it will be easier to deal with the temporary misery you may be enduring.

In the beginning, when I was starting my private practice, I didn't have money to hire staff. I had to do all the website work, and I had to make all the sales, I had to do all the training, I had to do all the writing of the manual. I had to do all the bookkeeping, I had to do all the brochure creation, and I wasn't good at everything. I was mediocre at half of it. I learned to outsource it as I started to make more money and put the right people in the right seats on the bus.

If you have the right people on the bus, in the right seats, and you know what direction the bus is going, you'll be very successful. But it takes a village to build a company just like it takes a village to raise a child. It may take you gathering several people around you to make you successful at what it is you've chosen to do, not just you out there flying solo.

If you don't have a plan, and this is most people, then yes, it will suck mightily, and it will be likely to fail, and this is what often leads to depression, frustration, anger, addiction, and worse.

Finally, one of the hurdles which will prevent people from attaining their goals is when they don't see the path or the signs when it is in front of them.

At the start of the chapter, I spoke of "discovery," and I think most people feel that if they landed in the right spot, they would discover something because it would be right there.

Everything we know existed before it was "discovered" by someone. It's not just putting yourself in the right place at the right time. That's part of it, sure, but you must know what you're looking for, so when you see it, you recognize the treasure.

You can discover what you want to do. You can find which direction you want to go, but now you have to create the person you want to be, and it can't just be the fake Facebook persona. You have to build the person from the inside out. If you like yourself on the inside, you're going to like yourself on the outside.

*"Someday" is not a day of the week.*

People say all the time, "I'll get to that someday." (My mother's notorious for that.)

Someday I'll fix that. Someday I'm going to do it, and someday I'll work out. Someday I'll change careers. What happens is you turn 40, then 50, then 60, and "someday" never comes.

~

*Sometimes people get stuck when they have not completed finding their authentic self. They'll do what they think is right, especially if told they're supposed to do something or follow a particular path.*

*Maybe they become an attorney. I have a client that only became an attorney because his Dad was an attorney, and his Grandfather was an attorney, and he heard that was what he was supposed to do, become an attorney.*

*He was a terrible attorney because he hated his job. But, he had just enough motivation to show up to work every day and grind through it.*

*And what he wanted was to be a Christian pastor. His family was Jewish, so they were utterly shocked.*

*His family asked, "How could you not want to be an attorney? And worse yet, you want to be a religion that we don't support."*

*He ended up becoming a part of the Christian council and a pastor. And he succeeded doing it very well, but his family turned their back on him. They were horrible.*

*A widespread mistake when finding your purpose is to keep doing what you're doing even when you don't like it and say, "This will get better. It will get better." That's a common mistake.*

*My client found the strength to break free of being stuck, even though it cost him a deep connection with his family, he gained his purpose.*

~

I see people being afraid to try new things and to shift, thinking that they must somehow come up with their purpose out of thin air instead of discovering it. By trying different things, you might suddenly stumble upon something that you enjoy. You wouldn't have known it just thinking about it. You must experience it, right?

When I was growing up, I didn't know what I wanted to do. I knew I was going to study psychology, and what I wanted to do was become an FBI agent.

I went to college, and I volunteered to be one of those Teacher's Assistants, and I hated it. I said, "Okay, that sucks." I knew right away that it wasn't going to work.

But I liked the teaching part. And then I wanted to be an FBI agent. I went, and I met one of the top female FBI agents at that time, and she said, "I have some advice for you."

Then she asked me, "Do you want to make money?"

I said, "Absolutely."

And she replied, "Don't become an FBI agent."

"Why?"

"Because you're going to make $20,000 a year fetching coffee. You're a woman."

She said, "Otherwise, you'll be doing undercover narcotics stings dressed as a prostitute."

I thought to myself, "Okay, this is not my purpose. It doesn't align with my authentic self because my authentic self wants to make money."

I graduated with my bachelor's degree, and I worked in a runaway shelter for girls. And then, from there, I worked in a nonprofit, long-term treatment center for women with children that was government-funded.

That non-profit job almost killed me. There was no AC in the summer. I had no perks, no health insurance, and I was broke all the time. I was putting in 80-hour workweeks, and we were called the working poor.

The women that lived there had money and supplies from the government. They had welfare, they had WIC for children, and they had health insurance. They had free housing, even free education. They had everything that I didn't have, and I was working my ass off, and I could barely pay my rent.

I knew that's what I didn't want to do.

Then I went and worked in a boys' home called Church Farm School, which was for rich kids who were almost bad kids. I learned that even though they had a shit ton of money, they still were crazy as the people who had no money.

So, I said, "Okay, maybe none of this is my purpose." And I studied yoga and Pilates and went to the gym.

I was 29, and I packed up everything I owned in my car, and I drove from Pennsylvania to Dallas, Texas.

I started at a fitness company with no money, literally, no money. I put my rent on a credit card and flipped over one of those plastic totes (the kind you store your Christmas stuff in), and on it I put my old computer from Walmart, which barely worked, and started running a fitness company. I had no idea what I was doing. I had a business partner who had some sales background, and we grew it to the largest fitness company in the world at that time. I don't think anyone ever surpassed us to this day.

We lost everything in the economic downturn in 2007. I ended up in a house with no heat and no running water, sitting there re-evaluating my purpose. I was 33 and feeling like I hadn't figured out who I was and where I was going.

Your purpose may change throughout your life because of the events in which you are involved. After I lost everything, we said, "What are we going to do?"

And my business partner says, "Let's start a music company. That sounds fun."

So, we did, we started an artist development company, helping musicians and budding artists hone their look online. It was very tiresome, and they were even more broke than us.

But the upside was that I met my husband! So the purpose of that company was for me to find my partner.

I met my husband after I manifested him. I was sitting in Laguna Beach, and I had no money. I was literally down to $300 in my bank account. And I sat down, and I said, "I think it's time for a husband."

I made a list of everything I wanted, everything I wanted to create in my world. I put my husband on that list and met him two months later in New York City.

~

**DO THIS**: Create a list of what you want and focus on it every single day. Every person, every situation you desire, put on that list so you can manifest your destiny. Post it on your mirror and places where you will see it and read it repeatedly.

~

But then after I met my husband, I said, "You know what, I'm going to take a break from creating my self and discovering my purpose and just have some fun."

I had spent ten years trying to figure out what I'm supposed to be doing and not enjoying life.

So that became, "I'm just going to enjoy life."

So, I did.

For a year, I just did everything with him that's fun, and it wasn't expensive stuff. It's not like we flew around the world. We literally would walk around New York City and look at the lights. We did that.

We would do fun things. And in New York City, we had no money. We had a $40 budget for fun every single week, and we had a blast.

It became a game of "How much fun can we create out of $40?" That, in itself, is fun. We would buy chicken salad and a couple of coffees, and walk around with a Diet Coke and gin, enjoying the hell out of the City.

And that's what we did. It was just fun, and it was enjoyable. And we weren't creating anything. I was learning how to be, learning how to be with him, and without constantly being in manifestation. Just learning to "be" was authentic in that moment.

From there, it became, "Okay. What am I supposed to be doing now? What's next?" And that's the problem. I think as a society, we feel we're always supposed to be doing something and figuring something out, that we never stop and listen.

And that's when I stopped, and I listened, "Okay, I'm going to see what happens."

I made a list of things that I enjoy doing and the list of things I didn't enjoy doing.

As I did that, I said, "You know, I think I'm called to go back into the addiction field."

I decided to get a job, despite not liking to work for other people. I thought that's the best way to get back into it, and so that's what I did. I sent out 80 job applications. I got three offers, none of which I wanted, but I took one, and I took a pay cut to $42,000/year to work 80 hours a week in the addiction industry to get my feet back into it. I didn't want to do that, but at that point, I had to do that financially.

Sometimes creating and manifesting what you want, which for me at the time was private practice, took that year of me buckling down at 42 grand to get back into it, to get my feet wet, to feel like I was going to be able to offer something in the private practice.

~

Sailing a little wooden ship to the New World is no different than you trying to figure out who you should be or what you should be doing.

Your "New World" is out there for you to discover and manifest as you create your reality. You must assemble your skills and desires and likes, set out onto some seas which could get rough, and keep the faith that you will succeed no matter what. And you will.

And along the way, you will discover new things about the world around you, about your relationships, and yourself. And, you will find who you are and what you should be doing.

~

**DO THIS**: Head on over to www.UnpauseYourLife.com if you haven't yet and tell us how you are doing?

I want to hear the results of your personality test and your conclusions. Did you learn anything, any personal insights? Are you currently doing something you shouldn't be doing? Has the test helped inform you of what you should be doing?

~

# CHAPTER THREE

# FINDING MY TRIBE

*Where Do I Fit?*

If you're the smartest person in the room, you're in the "wrong room."

I say that to all my clients. You should not be the smartest person in the room because if you are, you're in the wrong place. So, where do I belong? Where are my people? With whom do I resonate with and feel comfortable?

It is essential to know who your "people" are and knowing where to find them. It's important because we need to recognize "energy vampires," the people that drain you.

Unfortunately, these "vampires" are all too common, and we often put up with their negativity for far too long. We need to recognize toxic people. These are the people that are always complaining, they call you and have some drama unfolding in their world, and for some reason, they feel you need to have it in your world too. These people want to see you fail, if not outwardly, then deep inside themselves they don't want to see you succeed. Because if you do well, they will feel bad.

I am guessing you have some of these people in your life, we all do, often it's someone in your family so you can't just ghost them. We have names for them, descriptive names, like "energy drainers" and "drama queens."

I'm telling you right now; these are not your tribe; these are not your people. However, they're in your world right now because they are family, you either tolerate them, or you feel you've been friends with them for 20 years. You don't want to kick them out of your current tribe, but they're not helping you.

The people in your tribe currently that are not there for your highest good must go. I got rid of my entire tribe at one point and had to start over because I looked around me and said, these people are going nowhere. They do nothing with their lives. One plays Xbox and has no job. Out he goes. They might be one of your best friends, but if they're 35 years old and they're hanging out, just laying around playing games all day, they're not going to better you because they won't better themselves. People who better themselves will want to bring you up as a tribe. If they're holding you back, they have to go.

It's harder with family, but again, you need to find a way to spend less time with these "vampires" or toxic people and more time with people who challenge, inspire and have a positive influence on you. It would be best if you moved away from the drama and towards those who will help you reach your highest good.

There are three types of people in the world:

1. Those who make things happen.
2. Those who watch things happen.
3. And those who wonder what just happened.

You want to be in the first group, and you want to surround yourself with the movers and shakers that make things happen.

I want you also to be aware of the "fake tribe." These are people that you build relationships with on social media that aren't real. They are always posting how amazing their life is and all the fun things they do, but their life sucks. It's full of challenges, the ups, and downs we all face.

What they portray on social media, that's their non-authentic self. They have a fake persona. We get caught up in that as their real life. It's kind of like believing that "Reality TV" is real, it's not. For example, let's look at a Kim Kardashian selfie. That's not a selfie. She has a makeup artist, a hairstylist, a professional photographer, and three or five other people. Add in a little photoshop and facetune and more apps to change the shape of her face and thin her waist, and you have the photo. This photo may take a few hours, and a few hundred poses before the 'right' shot is posted on social media.

Moreover, she passes it off as a selfie. So people think, "I can do that, too."

No, you can't because that's not a selfie. That's not real. That's fake. We all fall into this trap at some point, and we buy into an artificial society.

You must go back to your authentic self here and find the authentic tribe, one that resonates with who you are and where you want to go.

The first thing that you must focus on is knowing who you are. That's number one.

We covered this earlier, and I've given you some great exercises to help you discover your self and your purpose. If you haven't found the answers to those questions yet, it is going to make it very difficult to find your tribe and recognize them when you do find them.

**DO THIS:** How to attract your tribe?

Ask and answer these questions:

- What am I looking for in my tribe? List qualities and traits.
- Where can I find these people?
- Is this a tribe of friends, or is it business-related?
- Am I looking for a significant other? Because that's different from looking for my tribe. That's a romantic relationship, and that's not what this book's about, so make sure that's not the situation.

- Where is my tribe, do I need them to be local, national, or international, depending on what I'm doing?

~

Next, when you start looking to build your connections with those who will lift you and help you develop your business, you will find your tribe at live, in-person events.

You will find your tribe at work, and you will find your tribe through your customers and your customer's connections and links.

You will see these people in school if you are a student.

These are reciprocal people. You give to them, and they give to you. The more you help and provide support to others, the more you will see it returned to you.

Where to find your tribe? Everywhere is the answer. Talk to everybody. When you rent a car at Alamo, talk to the person at the Alamo. They could be a client, and they could give you a client. These people could be your tribe, and you will only know if you get out there and meet strangers.

Getting out of your comfort zone and meeting strangers can be difficult for people, especially if they tend to be introverted, I get it. However, you can go to networking events, Meetup events, or Facebook events, and you may not know anyone. So, guess what? Everyone there may be in the same boat, you are all there to meet each other, to try new things, to learn, to connect, to build and grow.

~

*There are three kinds of fish in the sea: "Dolphins, Sharks, and Tuna."*

*Tuna fish are food. They don't know that the blood in the water is their own. They think everything that happens to them is somebody else's fault. They take no responsibility for their choices.*

*It's like there are three kinds of people: the people that make things happen, the people that watch things happen, and the people who say, "What happened?" (Those are the tuna.)*

*Sharks are eating machines. It's not their fault; they were born that way. But their job is to eat you. If you find yourself in the water with a shark, put your shark fin on or get out of the water. It's very difficult for a dolphin to act like a shark, and you'll never be as good at it as a real shark, so I recommend getting out of the water.*

*Dolphins are wonderful creatures: intelligent, happy, and playful. They communicate; they swim in schools. They've been known to ward off a shark attack and protect the other fish. They are fun-loving and beautiful, arcing in grace. Who are the fish in your sea?*

*Sharks will steal your money, and tuna will leech money from you. Real money is made when you have dolphins on your team.*

*Swim with the Dolphins, avoid Sharks and Tuna.*

*— Chellie Campbell*

~

I knew someone who would do random Facebook events, going to group meetings and events with which he had no idea about or previous experience. He was doing it to get out of his "comfort zone." We all live in a "comfort zone" of sorts. We get up, and we get in our cars, we go to work, we drive home. Maybe we go to the store or the gym, but we tend to go to the same places, see the same people. It's comfortable, we know it, and yet there is an entire world happening all around us.

People or groups post these events on Facebook, and he would see them. Then he would show up at these events or meetups, and they'd ask, "Who are you?" He met some amazing people through that and learned some cool things.

Also, almost every time, when he would show up, everyone was very welcoming.

They would say, "Yeah, come on in and join. You're not part of our group, but we don't care."

You never know where you're going to find your tribe. You need to get out there, get out of your comfort zone to find a clan with which you connect.

For example, if you have a dog, one of the easiest ways to find a tribe of friends or people that you can hang out with, is to go to a dog park. If you go there on a Saturday morning or after work and let your dog run around, you will be with other people who will likely be part of your "tribe," right? Because dog people are attracted to dog people. We like each other, and it's almost as if we love dogs more than we like people!

I met an excellent neighbor just by walking my dogs and found out that she ran a rescue. So, the next thing you know, we're talking about building an animal rescue. All because she was walking her dog and I was walking mine, and we ran into each other on the street. We weren't even at a dog park. We were simply walking down the road.

Motivational speaker Jim Rohn famously said that we are the average of the five people with whom we spend the most time. I have always said, "Show me your five closest friends, and I'll tell you who you are."

This philosophy relates to the law of averages, which is the theory that the result of any given situation will be the average of all outcomes.

**DO THIS:** List your five closest friends and answer these questions:

- What are their traits, and for what are they known?
- Are they known for not working, or do they have $10 an hour jobs?
- Are they succeeding in life?
- Are they executives?
- Who is in your "top five" circle?

~

When it comes to relationships, we are greatly influenced — whether we like it or not — by those closest to us. It affects our perceptions of the world around us, our way of thinking, our self-esteem, and our decisions.

Naturally, everyone is their own person, but research has shown that we are directly affected by our environment, often more than we think.

While it's ideal to be closely surrounded by positive, supportive people who want you to succeed, it's also necessary to have your critics. According to a study in the Journal of Consumer Research, "Tell Me What I Did Wrong: Experts Seek and Respond To Negative Feedback," novices have a preference for positive feedback, but experts want negative feedback so that they can make progress.

Also, the more successful you become, the more criticism you'll face. Glenn Llopis over at Forbes wrote about how "6 Types of People Build Your Mental Toughness," including doubters, critics, and the envious. Without them, you'd never sharpen your skills or develop your tough skin.

It takes a while to develop a skill where you don't allow other people's opinions of you to affect you and roll off like water on a duck's back. I get harassed by people spewing what I call "Haterade" constantly. I am sure someone will even have an issue with a positive and motivational book like this one!

Any successful person is going to have not only supporters but also those who, for reasons of their own, don't like what you are doing. You have to remember this is about their lack of achievements, not your ability to succeed.

> *"Your opinion of me is none of my business."*
>
> *– Nikki Sixx*

They don't want you to succeed because it makes them look or feel bad. Also, these people may end up having to compete with you for the same market share. Sadly, they end up internalizing things about you that they shouldn't.

I have dealt with people posting negative things online that are not true, or calling my press outlets, trying to get me kicked off. Calling the radio stations, I'm supposed to be on and telling people that I shouldn't be on there just because they don't like me. People think they're bigger than they are, and think they have more clout or more weight just because they fear you.

Don't let these people slow you down. Let their negativity fuel your energy and resolve to take yourself even further.

Most people are afraid to leave their comfort zone, their home in their city, to seek experiences in different communities, whether it's within the state or the country, or traveling around the world. It's more often than not because they have developed a preconceived notion or judgment about a place without ever having been there themselves.

People ask me all the time, "How do you live in Miami? Nobody speaks any English, nobody is from America, and it's violent."

I say, "Are you kidding me? It's beautiful. People are nice, and the food is fabulous, the culture is amazing. There are people from all different cultures here. Yes, Spanish is the primary language, but so is Russian, and French. So is English, and it's nice to be in such a diverse city that's still part of America yet feels like a whole different country."

Also, these same people respond, "It's a third-world country."

No, it's not. There's nothing third-world about Miami. It's like New York, but clean. People have heard bad things about it.

"I'm not coming down there. You might get mugged or raped," I've had people tell me. You are more likely to get mugged or raped in my hometown than you would in Miami.

It's not just about living somewhere different either, and I understand that can be a change that is just too overwhelming for most people. It's expensive to move and should be something you save up for, so it becomes an exciting adventure, not a stressful and anxious endeavor.

However, one thing you can do is to travel more, to explore, to find new places and people to interact with along the way.

Europeans travel all the time because it's part of their culture. You get packed up, and you visit, you go on vacation. If you're from Germany, you vacation in France, and then you go to Switzerland. When I lived in Pennsylvania, our vacation was down the Jersey Shore.

Every year for one week, my mother dragged us to Jersey. We didn't have enough money, so we cooked food in the room on a frying pan, and then we would hang out on the beach. I never realized how dark and cold the water was until I swam on South Beach.

I hate New Jersey for that exact reason.

To this day, that's her vacation.

She tells me, "I'm going to go on vacation."

"Where are you going?" I ask.

"The shore."

"How about Vegas?"

"No, no," she replies.

"How about anywhere else besides New Jersey."

She's adamant, "No, that's where we go because it's a tradition. It's culture. It's what we do."

She came down to Florida for my wedding, "I could never live here."

I said, "You've been here twice. How could you know you'll never live here? It's a huge state."

My Mom is comfortable, and she likes her small, familiar tribe in her small hometown. It works for her. She knows where she fits, and she is happy. For me, I needed a bigger tribe. A tribe that thought globally, not just locally.

People get stuck, and they get comfortable with their current tribe. But sometimes we outgrow our tribe.

~

**DO THIS:** Have you outgrown the tribe you're in, and can you add new people?

It can be uncomfortable to have somebody new in your tribe, but you can have many tribes. You can have different people for different things. You might have people who are in your "work" tribe or people who are your "friends" tribe. Maybe you've heard someone say, "I have a husband and a work husband."

You can have multiple people in your tribe or many tribes.

List some of your different tribes.

List who is in them.

Have you outgrown them?

~

Also, many people are scared to go somewhere new. What are the terrible things that happen? What if I go to Spain and I don't know how to order food because I can't speak Spanish? What if this happens or what if that happens? It's always "what if."

I encourage you to travel and get outside your comfort zone. It doesn't have to be far, and it doesn't have to be expensive.

Look at your "Bucket List," are there places you want to go, things you want to see or do? You would be amazed at how cheaply you can travel if you plan it out, maintain some flexibility in your schedule, and search for discounts.

My husband and I made our whole trip to Alaska on a thousand bucks. That blows people's minds: two round-trip tickets, four nights, car rentals, all the food, a thousand dollars.

I saved the points on my credit card for a year. I had repeated stays at Hilton, which gave us discounted rates when we stayed at the Hilton, for example.

Your entire journey does not have to be a Ritz-Carlton experience. It just has to *be*.

I met many fun people on my trip up to Alaska. I had a great time and connected with a lot of interesting people to whom I still talk. Traveling can always help you meet new people, especially if you're in an area where you have to speak. If you take a cruise, if you're on an airplane, these are places you have to meet people. You could sit there with your headset on and ignore them, but if you're trying to find a tribe, everybody could be in your tribe.

Talk to them. Find out who they are.

~

*I thought I had found my tribe. I had worked with someone in a partnership to make some new and incredible supplements.*

*She sent me a text two weeks ago and said, "I'm selling the supplement line without you."*

*I said, "What?"*

*We had a contract to develop this line of supplements and sell them together, next thing I know I'm getting the message, "I'm selling your supplement with somebody else."*

*Soon she's got a website, and she's selling OUR supplement line without me.*

*I thought she was my tribe. She is what I would call a "Wolf in Sheep's Clothing," and they are out there. Beware and don't be too trusting of strangers, they may turn out to be toxic.*

*Give people the benefit of the doubt but take care of yourself and learn from your mistakes. I sure have.*

*Brandon Novak is a professional skateboarder, actor, stuntman, and friend of Bam Margera and is a prominent member of the CKY Crew. Novak made several appearances in the CKY videos, Bam's Haggard films, and the Jackass films.*

*Novak, along with co-author and CKY filmographer Joseph Frantz, authored his first book titled Dreamseller (2008) based on his life and experiences with heroin in Baltimore. A movie of the same name was supposed to be in production but was stopped when Novak began using heroin again.*

*When Novak was 14, he was a professional skateboarder on the Powell Peralta Team, but lost his spot due to what he says was a long bout with "psychoactive substance abuse."*

*In 2010, Novak was arrested at Chester County Hospital for an outstanding warrant after being admitted for breaking several bones filming a scene for Jackass 3D. He was charged with forging a prescription after he tried to pass a fake prescription for Xanax.*

*After a string of relapses and homelessness, Novak has been clean and sober since March 20, 2015.*

*In September 2016, he finally found a healthy and supportive tribe when he began working for Banyan Treatment Center in Pompano Beach, Florida.*

*He now uses his story to help and inspire others to find success in sobriety. He's spoken to high school kids and policymakers about the realities of drug and alcohol use. He has completely changed whom he surrounds himself with and finds meaning in his work.*

*"My name is Billie Lee, and I am transgender. I was born and raised as a boy. As a child, I was forced to play the male role: "Billie, only sissies walk like that." I honor my parents for what they knew. They were only trying to protect me with the knowledge they were given. After being taken in and out of school, misdiagnosed with childhood depression and OCD, my parents just assumed I would turn out gay...*

*...After leaving my hometown and discussing my gender identity issues with a therapist, I immediately started the physical transformation, which began with lots of hormones and ended with major surgeries. During any transformation in life, you are vulnerable, like an open wound just waiting to heal. Most trans people, including myself, deal with a lot of bullying, which I thought would be over after high school. However, during my awkward transformational stages, I was beaten up by society. I couldn't get a job for over a year, and dating was not even an option. I felt all the doors close, and it was extremely lonely.*

*...As the healing ended, and I was forced to face the world as me, Billie Lee, a beautiful woman, I was so shocked at all the possibilities. Every door just opened for me, and it was as if the red carpet was rolled out. Job opportunities were everywhere, and*

*boys were lined up. I thought, "Wow, society finally accepts me! I've finally made it!" I walked around, and still do, amazed by what my beauty does for me. As society accepted me as a woman, I thought, "This is the dream! I'm finally the cool kid on the block." No one questioned anything."*

*~ itsmebillielee.com*

~

Just like you, I have had many failed relationships. Also, friendships that come and go. However, I always try to take these experiences and learn from them and think about what I can implement to make myself a better person.

Moreover, think to yourself, "What can I use from that broken relationship or fractured friendship to restructure what I'm looking for in my tribe?"

I know that this can shift and change over time because what I needed when I was 20 years old is going to be much different as I age. Even in a romantic relationship, your desires for a hot and sexy partner changes over time to prefer conversation over coffee while sitting on the front porch.

~

**DO THIS:** Go to different events, some random and some in alignment with exactly what you are looking for in a tribe. Collect business cards and phone numbers to connect with these people later. If you are looking to find people that enjoy kayaking find a MeetUp that does kayaking, but also consider maybe a running club or a food tasking group. Open your horizons for new experiences.

~

We all know people from high school who are still friends with the same people from high school, right? Maybe it's a couple of girls or guys you hung out with in high school, and one got pregnant in high school. Now they have five kids with five different partners, never been married, and they never moved. Or maybe you've got another friend that ended up in jail and is a drug addict. I had friends like this, and I had to let them all go, to grow. Sometimes people are afraid to get rid of the friends around them, to grow. Their current friends know them, accept them, and as social creatures, we like that feeling of connection.

I didn't have a lot of close friends in high school. I had probably three good friends that, to this day, don't judge me or treat me any differently even though I've been successful, more successful than they have. They treat me just like they did when I was in high school. I was often looked down upon because I was poor, and I kept to myself at high school. I didn't have any money and didn't have any clothes, and I felt very insecure. I had the same five outfits that I rotated every week and two pairs of shoes, that's it.

I'm thriving now, and a lot of them are not successful. A lot of them have divorced and have retail jobs. The people that made fun of me and laughed at me and who are not successful are not my tribe. Those are not people I want to revisit or rehash.

However, there are people from high school that are still friends, and they all still hang out together, and they yet haven't made it. They're doing the same things, working in the same retail jobs they did in high school. There is nothing wrong with this; they are all in the same tribe. However, I am in a whole different tribe because I have different goals and dreams. I had to move on to a new tribe.

Your tribe or circle of influencers will change over time, as do your needs. It's essential to embrace this transformation and movement, and it will allow you to let go of toxic people because they hinder your growth. Also, if someone isn't growing with you, stuck in a world that's dragging them down, you need to cut the ties and move onward and upward.

~

**DO THIS:** Head on over to TheMoneyMastermindclub.com. We have a tribe. You might belong here, check it out and join us for our Mastermind group!

**DO THIS:** I want to hear about your networking experiences. Have you decided to move away from some of your close friends because they are holding you back? Please share your thoughts, we'd love to hear!

**DO THIS:** Write a 30-second elevator pitch to use to meet your tribe. This is just a quick introduction you can use with your name, what you do (or like to do), and what you are looking for. Need help? Our marketing course has this for you! Head over to Unpauseyourlife.com

**DO THIS:** Head over to Complete the Circle Of Influence Exercise to hone your tribe seeking skills and learn which "Energy Vampires" and Toxic People need to be removed for you to find your Success Tribe!

Head over to www.UnpauseYourLife.com and download the Form!

# CHAPTER FOUR

# MONEY

*Knowing and Understanding My Worth*

I was raised to believe that I was undeserving of money or the beautiful things and experiences that you can obtain by having money. Shopping at the flea market and the thrift store was a big deal and a big shopping outing for my family. My mother would always tell us, "you don't need that" or "we can't afford that trip, or those new shoes."

My mother received child support for us from my father, and we would get new clothes twice a year, spring and fall. She would save up that money and take us on a shopping trip to the local mall (not the expensive one in King of Prussia). Now we didn't get Benetton, Express, Gap, and Izod like the rest of the kids. We got to shop at DebJoy and Payless Shoes. We even shopped at Kmart (this is way before Walmart). We received $200 to spend, and we were told **that it was lots of money.**

This money lack mentality instilled in me at a young age that small amounts of money were a lot, and we could not obtain large amounts. Vacations were not an option. Remember how I told you that we went every year to the Jersey Shore and stayed in a cheap motel, and my mother would cook all the meals in the room on a hot plate? We never ate out, being told that it was a luxury for the rich. Simple things like going out for breakfast after Sunday church were out of our financial reach.

My mother would remind us that" a week's worth of groceries quickly equals one restaurant meal, and we didn't have that kind of money to burn."

Sometimes your family of origin will tell you that money is the root of all evil, which I feel is not uncommon. Maybe you were told you shouldn't ask for money or want money because money is bad.

Money is not the root of all evil. The actual quote from the Bible says, "The love of money is a root of all kinds of evil, for which some have strayed from the faith in their greediness and pierced themselves through with many sorrows" (I Timothy 6:10). This passage is saying that the love of money is the issue at hand here, not money itself.

I'm here to tell you money is not bad. Money is merely the universal exchange for products and services. It's energy. That's all it is. That's it. If you have had this code hammered into you, that money is evil; then you must change your perception.

**Perception is your reality**. If you perceive you're broke, then you're broke. If you perceive you're wealthy, you're wealthy. How you feel about money dictates how much is in your bank account. Now, if you want to rent a $4000 a month condo in Miami and you work at Burger King for $10.00 an hour, it will take more than perception to get you to a financial goal to rent that condo. You will need action, as well. However, for now, let's talk about the perception of money.

My husband could care less about money. He tells everybody, "I don't care about money, and I just want to have fun."

His bank account is in the negative more than it's positive because he doesn't care about money.

Then he's married to me who's extremely money focused. He'll call me, "I need money."

I ask, "I just gave you $100, what did you spend it on?"

"I don't know..."

He bought a lottery ticket. He bought a bracelet, whatever shiny object got his attention, he bought. He doesn't think that he spent his entire amount on garbage, he assumes more will come. He has no value for money, even though he loves to spend it! Because he doesn't think about it, because he's not money focused. How he feels about money, which means he doesn't care about it, is fully reflected in his bank account.

Empty.

If you don't like money, you will always be broke. If you fear money, you will be broke. If you are afraid to make money, you will always be broke. However, it is not evil. It is a necessary commodity to exchange the things you need and the things you want.

If you want to live somewhere nice, or you want to make sure you have food, and the lights are always on, you need money. If you are currently thinking, "I'm having trouble wanting money," and you change it into, "I don't want to have my lights shut off, and I don't want my house taken from me." It's about how to change your perception.

We must make peace with money because we tend to have an unhealthy relationship with money. If you hoard it, you get less of it. I like to think of it as energy. It should flow in and flow out. It's ebb and flow.

You get people who make loads of money and then hold onto it. I have a client who had made $750K off Bitcoin. What did he do? He hoarded it.

What happened? He lost half of it because he hoarded it. His ex-wife took it.

I asked, "Well, why don't you spend it? Why not use it?"

Money is energy. You can't hoard it, but you also can't just throw it out the window. It would help if you learned how to make peace with it. Then it would be best if you learn the value of it. What is the value of money? I don't mean $1 versus $100. I mean, what does wealth give you? It gives you opportunities. It gives you freedom. It provides you peace of mind.

If you are in the service industry and you want to help the most people, you charge a larger amount of money for services so you can donate your time to those that cannot afford you. That is right. You charge more for your time because time is the most valuable thing you have.

One of the best lines I ever heard was, "It is easier to cry in a BMW than on a Bicycle." You have to open your mind that you can and will make money, and you need to. You also need to know your worth, which we will talk more about in this chapter.

I decided a long time ago that I wanted to be free. I don't want to be stuck in an office nine to five, Monday to Friday. That's not free. That's making someone else money, building their dreams, and making them rich.

Right now, as I work on this book, I'm taking two hours out of my day to sit at the pool, not making money, but banking my efforts for a possible reward later. That is creating abundance. I am putting in the work hours (even at the pool at noon on a Tuesday) to get the job done that will bring in abundance.

One of my favorite authors, Chellie Campbell, has always said you need to bring in ships and focus on creating abundance. You can not just think about it, and you have to do the work behind it. So sitting by the pool and creating my mantra "money flies at me from all directions" is only step one. Now I need to 'send out ships' as Chellie says and watch them come in ripe with the bounty!

This way of thinking about wealth is the money mindset principle. The money mindset principle is one that supports my belief that I can create money, and I use the law of attraction to create my abundance. I find this sometimes freaks people out, but when I go to the mall, for example, I envision a parking spot up front. "Rock Star Parking" is unheard of, there's never a front parking spot at the mall, especially at Christmas time. If you can find any place to park at the mall the week before Christmas, it is an act of God. Unless you know how to **speak it into existence**. So now this is where I get all metaphysical on you because it works.

At Christmas time, I will get a front-row parking spot every time I go to the mall, and people ask, "How did you do that?"

It's all in mindset. I don't allow any negative thoughts in, and I say, "I'm going to get that spot." I focus on visualization that the spot is open and waiting for me, inevitably, a car will pull out, and I will be next in line.

It's all about creation. Thinking I have and then focusing on my mantra, "Money and big clients fly at me from all directions, or in this case, parking spots, and I simply create what I need."

Keep in mind you may not get the front row, you may get ten rows back, but ten rows back is better than no spot at all or parking three football fields away.

~

**DO THIS:** Do you have a "Money Mantra?" Create one keeping these mantra tips in mind:

- Make it a phrase you'd say and use. No stilted, Shakespearean language unless that's how you speak daily. Slang is welcome.

- Make it positive. Use positive and specific phrasing. Don't say: One day I am going to have a full book of clients, or I hope to have an entire book of clients, I wish I had a full book or too general terms like I need more clients. Get specific: "I need ten new clients by the end of the month."

- Use your mantra consistently. Unlike some things which, when overused, lose efficacy - mantras grow more powerful from use.

~

There was a time where I was sitting at my kitchen counter looking at my husband, and I said, "I just wrote a rent check I can't cash."

He glanced over and asked, "What do we do?"

I replied, "We're going to focus on money coming in, not going out."

We took several pieces of paper, and we wrote how much we wanted to cover our rent, and we put them all around the house. Within two days, I got a client that paid $3,200, plenty of money to cover our rent. He didn't trust the process and thought it was a joke until he watched me make it happen using the law of attraction, and when I invited him to try it with me, it blew his mind.

He decided he wanted to go back on tour (If you haven't read my first book *I Married a Junkie,* my husband is rock n roll drummer), and we started to discuss logistics.

We applied the money abundance and money mindset principles and the law of attraction mantras to his tour creation. We discussed logistics like what type of band (rock n roll), where (the USA and Europe), and even how much money he wanted to generate per show. The key is we were doing this together and agreeing on what we wanted as a team, and it made us twice as powerful in creation and manifestation.

I got 12 sheets of printer paper and a huge, fat black marker. We handwrote (no photocopying, as it changes the energy) that he will go on tour, he will make a certain amount per show, all food and expenses included, and we put the USA and Europe as locations with a time limit of 2 months from the date. It was in July. We then hung them all around the condo, on mirrors, on doors, above the bed, even put one in the car.

Then we focused on what we wrote on them. We set our intent daily and 6 to 10 times a day, just on the goal. While we were doing this, we needed to send out the ships Chellie talked about in her books. The legwork has to get done.

We took to google and hit up every contact we had ever made in the music business and started sending out his one-sheet and website.

Day one: Nothing

Day two: Nothing

Day three: Nothing

Day four, he is discouraged. "Keep on focusing," I tell him.

Day five, I got a weird LinkedIn email (from nothing I even sent out) that a band was looking to hire a drummer. I sent his one-sheet and his website. I googled them and realized they were in LA. Now mind you, we had limited funds, and we were in Miami, clear on the other side of the country. We didn't let that stop us. We would get it.

We focused, we sent a follow-up email, and his phone rang on day 7. They called to invite him out to LA for an audition. He was kind of stressing out, "Oh my god, this is going to require a round-trip ticket to LA!"

Keep in mind that we had no money, and a round trip ticket to LA was at least six hundred bucks.

I said, "We'll figure it out." That is the next step in law of attraction, it doesn't all just come to you, you have to look, you have to find, and you have to seek. You may even need to get creative to make it happen.

I logged into our credit card account and used points to send him to LA. It cost us nothing, and I even figured out to get the hotel for free.

I was able to "win our entire wedding." Yes, the entire thing, venue, food, DJ, and even the photographer, using these principles. Sometimes money is not just paper currency. It is goods and services that are worth money. When we wanted to get married in 2010, we did not have much money at all, we lived paycheck to paycheck, and sometimes our bank account was in the negative, we barely had enough to pay the bills.

So, I created our dream wedding. I even got my wedding dress for $75.00 (it was a beautiful sundress from Victoria Secret), and we held the wedding on the beach, and it was gorgeous. That is abundance in its purest form. Our entire wedding cost under $1,000.

Now when you are creating with the law of abundance, it may not be exactly what you envisioned, but it will be close, and it will be what you need. Keep an open mind and focus on the end game.

I dragged my now husband to every bridal show we could go to. We entered every giveaway, every contest, and looked for what we could afford. The beach wedding on St. Pete Beach was $149 per person, and that was just the food. You still had photographers, flowers, cake, and dresses. It was out of budget. I wanted that wedding, but I could not afford it. So, I set out to get what we needed.

We walked by Tina Ortiz photography, and she flagged us down. She said that my fiancée looked like Bret Michaels, and she loved Bret Michaels and wanted to offer us free photography (we just paid for her gas and hotel). They gave one couple each year this gift. We accepted, and I have amazing photos!

We entered a dinner contest for $40.00 and went to the event. There were ten couples, each one threw their ticket into a hat, and the owner drew a couple that would win DJ, food, venue, and dancing. We won. Even though we ended up going to the beach to get married, we won a full set up for 50 people. Exactly what we asked for when imagining our day.

So when my husband wanted to go on tour, he remembered the wedding creation we did, and we set the same powerful intentions for the music tour and him getting not only the audition but the offer.

He flew to LA to audition. He was up against some pretty famous touring drummers and household names, and he got the job. But not only did he get the gig, but it was also for the exact amount on our paper plus expenses, and it had a USA and Europe leg. Even crazier, he had to learn their music and was leaving in 2 weeks. We won, we created precisely what we asked for while manifesting. He came back, and he asked me, "How the hell did you do that?"

I said, "That's what I do. I create something from nothing. That's the law of attraction." I have built all of my companies using this process, and I even created meeting my husband using the fundamental principles of the law of attraction and money mindset. That is right, I made a list of exactly what I wanted when I wanted to take a husband (yes I call it that), and my list included: tattooed, pierced, fun, he loves to travel, didn't want any more kids) and I got everything on my list.

What's the catch?

You don't get everything you ask for, nor in the time you want it. You get what you need first, and if you are not ready to receive it, you won't get it either.

If it's not in line with my higher purpose, the Universe will not allow me to have it. That means if I say, "I want an Aston Martin," which is a $500,000 car or, "No, a McLaren," and I post pictures of a McLaren all around and it's not aligned with my higher purpose, the Universe will not respond with a new vehicle. Meaning, I already have a car. I have a great car. I happen to own three vehicles and an RV, and I don't need another. The Universe will not give me that McLaren.

However, if I say, "I need to figure out how to make money this month because I have the staff to pay and I want to do something extra, like publish a book or launch a new course," then the Universe will provide. I am asking for higher purpose items, not just material things that are shiny and pretty. Or fast, like a McLaren.

Universe will let you play with it, but you must be ready to receive it. If you ask for more money, yet you throw pennies in the trash because you deem them worthless or too much work to count, you are sending a mixed message to the Universe. You want money, but you throw it away. Universe will not, in turn, give you more money then.

I talk to the Universe; I ask for what I need and explain how I will use it for a higher good. It comes in strange ways, I focus on money flying at me from all directions, and maybe I will send out some emails and do some marketing, and the phone will ring. Some of you will pray to God, some of you will tap into a higher power, and it is all the same thing, an energy greater than us that we can tap into to make things happen.

This is how crazy this is, typically when I have this conversation with the Universe, about a week later maybe I'll get a phone call from one of the treatment centers I have trained, and they need to pay me, right now.

They'll say, "We have to use grant money because if we don't, we have to pay taxes on it, and if we don't use all the grant money, they don't allow us anymore." So just like that, I get what I need to get going on the new project.

I also get blessed when I give money away. Once I had only $10.00 left in my pocket. That is all I had until a payday, five days away. I wanted a coffee, and as I was walking into the coffee shop, I saw a homeless, starving man and his dog. I am a sucker for pets, so I bought him and the dog breakfast sandwiches and water. It was $9.98. I had no money for coffee for myself. As I was handing him the food, one of my coworkers had pulled up and saw me and said I am so happy that you are helping others, and I want to reward you. He bought me a coffee. It was the best coffee on the planet that day. When I give money away (it is universal energy that we use in exchange for goods and services), it flows back to me. If I hold on to it or hoard it, no more money flows my way.

Once you get what you wanted or needed (more important), now you must give thanks and pay it forward. Once, when I lived in Houston, I was down to my last $20, and I gave $10 of it to a homeless man, and I sent a message to the Universe asking to cover me, as I was almost out of money. Rent was due soon, and I asked for clients and focused on everyone giving me what I needed. I put business cards out everywhere, and I landed a new client the next day that bought $2500 of coaching. That is the catch, you must be grateful, and you must pay it forward, you cannot hoard money, you will not be granted any more.

I teach my clients how to do this, I teach my husband, and I'll show you. Everyone's response is generally, "This is insane." However, they do it, and it works.

I don't sit around and pray to God. I don't go to church. I say, "This is what I need to do," and if it's in alignment with my purpose and my higher good, Universe will provide it, and it always does.

That Universe doesn't just go, "Here's your money. Have a nice day!" Universe will say, "You have to go to Colorado for the week. You must fly into Denver and stay in a hotel. You have to leave your family to teach for five days consecutively to make some money. It will be bitter cold in January and you hate the cold, but here you go!"

I do it because Universe set it up. Some months I will be at home for only three days the entire month because Universe is providing. Sometimes it is quiet because Universe is giving me a break and gearing me up for the next abundance windfall. It's an ebb and flow of constant energy. I have no guaranteed income, no base salary. I start over each month at zero. That freaks many people out. How can you do that? Trust. Believe. Create.

It's a mindset, but it's even more than that, it's also when you are ready to do the work behind the mindset. It's not going to come for free, and it must be in alignment with your higher good and your purpose.

For me, the deal I made with this company when I talked to Universe, I said, "I promise if you let me get another big company going, I will make sure everybody I touch has money and abundance. Everybody is compensated, and everybody is compensated correctly for their work. Anyone that is in lack, I will help as much as I can, and I most certainly will send the elevator back down when I hit the top." Universe listened.

I've always been allowed to do that, and that goes along with my money mindset. I have always believed that if you skip a bill or you're trying not to pay something, you will lose three times the amount of money you tried to keep. I always write 'thank you' on my checks, and I am grateful that I can pay all my bills today. There was a time when I couldn't, and a time I was homeless. I wanted to pay my bills, and now I am thankful that I can. Gratitude is key. There will always be people that have more money than you, a more exceptional car, a more beautiful house, and a more fit body. You are not competing with any of them, only yourself to be better and more abundant than you were yesterday.

You must be at peace with the money you have or don't have. Also, when you are focusing on creating new wealth, do it from a place of goodness, not a place of anger, because if it comes from anger or deception or thievery, it will we be reversed on you three times.

If you tried to put negative energy out there and ruined somebody or a competitor, it will happen to you. So the rules of the game are to create from love, not negativity, be grateful, give back, focus, and do the work and it will work for you.

~

 **DO THIS:** Write down all the preconceived notions you have about money. Your list of fears and stopping blocks. For example, "I don't deserve money" or "money is the root of all evil." Once you make a list—reverse it and make it a positive. These will be your mantras. "Money is not the root of all evil; it is necessary and vital to life." Focus on these daily.

~

What is your Value?

What is your Worth?

Most people devalue what they have to offer or don't know their worth. They are afraid to ask for what they are worth and end up feeling empty, over-worked, and undervalued. How do you put a price tag on your worth?

Well, work backward! Start with your expenses and write it down, and that is the base number you need to meet each month. Add up the rent, car, phone, electric, credit cards, loans, and throw in a food and gas bill. This amount is the base you need to make each month to live. You're worth at least this much. Now add to it.

My rule of thumb is double your money. Double your expenses that are your base worth and go up from there. Now you have a starting point.

When I went into private practice, I started with a number, I was going to charge $125 per hour, and I doubled it. I got clients at that rate immediately. My mantra became, "My price is based on my talent, not your budget," and I stuck with that. I don't accept insurance, and I know my worth. I know what I can do, and I know that I am worth every penny a client will spend.

What is your worth?

~

*Actor and comedian Jim Carrey was a born entertainer. In school, his teacher let him perform his comedy routines for his classmates at the end of the day in exchange for being quiet during class. Carrey used to wear his tap shoes to bed, just in case his parents needed cheering up in the middle of the night.*

*When he was young, Carrey's father lost his job, and the whole family had to live in a camper van on a relative's lawn. They all took jobs working as janitors and security guards at a nearby factory -*

*Carrey himself worked an eight-hour shift straight after school.*

*Carrey got his start as a stand-up comedian at 15 when his father drove him to Toronto's Yuk Yuk's club. Wearing a yellow suit that his mother sewed, Carrey's debut bombed so badly that it gave him doubt whether he could make a living as an entertainer. Fortunately, he persevered and gained popularity as a stand-up comedian. A year later, he dropped out of high school to concentrate on his career.*

*At 19, Carrey headed to Hollywood - but like many young actors trying to make it in Tinseltown, he found that success was elusive. In 1985, a broke and depressed Carrey drove his old beat-up Toyota up the Hollywood hills. There, sitting overlooking Los Angeles, he daydreamed of success. To make himself feel better, Carrey wrote himself a check: $10 million for "acting services rendered," post-dated it ten years, and kept it in his wallet.*

*The check remained there until it deteriorated, but Carrey eventually made it: he earned millions for movies like Ace Ventura: Pet Detective and Dumb and Dumber. When his father passed away in 1994, Carrey slipped the check into the casket to be buried.*

~

**DO THIS:** I want to hear about your experiences with money, do you think it is the root of all evil? Check out our money mastermind tribe at this site below if you want more money, more freedom and more free time! Come over to www.TheMoneyMastermindClub.com

**DO THIS:** Create your worth and value. Grab a piece of paper or jot down right here the answers to these questions: What am I worth per hour? What is my value? What do I bring to the table? Also, what is holding me back? What is 'my price tag,' or what amount do I want to attract?

**DO THIS:** List all of your expenses: Rent/Mortgage, phone, internet/tv, electric, gas, food, make a spreadsheet. Are you spending on stuff that is a waste? Remove that!

What do you NEED to make per month? Then double it. That is your worth to start, and you can only go up from there!

# CHAPTER FIVE

# PERCEPTION IS REALITY

*Deconstructing a Limiting Belief System*

In this chapter, you're going to learn what a limiting belief system is and how to break that mentality. You're also going to learn how your perception becomes your reality and what a glass ceiling means.

We're going to cover different ways that your limiting belief system held you back in relationships and career and how to break down that wall and theoretically break through the glass ceiling.

So first let's talk about what is a limiting belief system. A limiting belief system is rooted most often in childhood. It is usually based on an approach where your parents (and the people that are raising you or in your immediate circle) convince you that they have done something for generations, and that's what you need to do as well.

For example, we sometimes see people having babies at age 16 going on Welfare, having more babies, and staying on Welfare. Their parents are on Welfare, and then their kids are on Welfare as well, because they're told or shown that's what we do.

The message and lessons they learn are, "You're not going to go to college, you're not going to finish high school. You're going to get pregnant, have babies, and get into the system."

This is a limiting belief system. We have done something a specific way for generations, and it shall continue simply because this is what we know.

In my specific case, I was told growing up that in my family, the women work in the hospital, or they work in some form of caretaking role where they help other people complete a medical task, like hospital work or working in a doctor's office. You don't go to college, and you find a 'good job' (one that is 40 hours a week with benefits), you then stay here until you retire.

Toss in their advice for your love life, which was to marry a local boy or at least one within a few towns over and start a family.

You move a few houses down from Mom or Dad, and you have this job, and your partner has their job, and you get pregnant and start popping out kids.

You do the kid thing, and you work, and you enjoy your Saturday running errands and your Sunday mowing the lawn, and then you go back to work on Monday and do it all over again. If you are lucky, you get to retire and travel around the country. IF you make it that far. And maybe, just maybe you get a gold watch for being with the company for a long, long time.

My grandmother worked at the hospital as a dietary supervisor, and then my mother worked at the hospital in the film file room. It was expected that I would get a job at the hospital. My grandmother lived in the same town she grew up in, right down the street from her family of origin and had two kids. Then my mother moved down the street from her and had her two babies. My sister moved down the street and had two kids. See the pattern?

Graduate high school, find a local boy, get married, pop out two kids, and live near the family unit.

I decided to break this limiting belief system. My perception was that this was not my reality. I was determined to do something different and follow a path of my choosing, not what was being "sold" to me by my family.

My first conversation to break this limiting belief system was over dinner with my mother and my stepfather. I told them that I wanted to go to college and get a degree in psychology. This was met with laughter and a stern talking of 'you don't need to go to college, girls like you don't need a degree.' My mother's entire plan for me was to get a job at the mall (after my failure at the hospital as a Candy Striper volunteer), work my way up to manager and buy a nice prefab home.

This didn't sit well with me.

I was NOT interested in staying in Pottstown, there is nothing to do there, and I certainly had no interest in working in a mall. My customer service skills are not so good. Let us say I would probably get fired after the first time I dropped the F-bomb. Knowing my personality, that would be in the first hour of having to do customer service.

I decided to go against the system. I wanted out. This small-time mentality was not for me. A local boy and a local job and a local house were not for me. I wanted to make something amazing of my life and travel all around the world and use a laptop and a cell phone to work (keep in mind back in the late 80's this was not even a reality yet).

I wanted to create my reality, and I broke free of the limiting belief system of all the women in our family. This belief, the one that told you to marry a local boy, move two streets down from Mom and Dad and have two kids just like every generation before, was not on my agenda.

I knew I could do it too; that is what freaked out the entire family. I was determined to create my reality.

I started by going to college and getting a Bachelor's Degree (no one even helped me fill out the paperwork or move in on-campus), then a Master's Degree and finally a Ph.D. I even hopped in the car, moved 2,700 miles away, and birthed a company instead of kids. I have written two books (this is number 3) and had five companies. I have seen every state and every national park in America. I bought an RV and lived in it and traveled for an entire year.

In the beginning, my family humored me, then as I grew and started doing TV appearances on NBC, CNN, KTLA, and more, they started to realize I wasn't coming back to live in the neighbored and work at the mall. It wasn't until I was in People magazine the second time that my mother finally realized I was living my dream, not hers.

Thankfully my sister provided the grandbabies, so I was off the hook on that one, although until I hit 40, it was the topic of discussion. So how did I 'escape' the lifestyle that was handed to me?

Well, first, I disregarded the limiting belief system by getting very clear on what I wanted and (didn't want) I knew "I could do something different."

Half the battle is knowing you can do it and not getting sucked in when your family or circle of friends wants to hold you back. I had to leave everything I knew and start over, and I loved every minute of it. Look at your circle right now, are you the smartest person? Then you are not in a circle; you are in a cage.

Think about that for a second. If you are caged up, you will never succeed. You will stay right where you are and be miserable. Sure, your friends and family will love to have you follow in their path, but is that what *YOU* want?

Or do you want *MORE?* If you said more, then keep reading, I am going to show you how to create and sustain it. You can have the life you want, and you can enjoy every minute of it. But you must get over a few hurdles first and tackle a few things.

One is perception.

Our perception of our reality can tie into our limiting belief system, and we can use it to continue the cycle. Think of a hamster wheel. Once the hamster is on the wheel going super-fast, he usually flies off. He doesn't know how to stop the wheel, and he gets on and does it over and over and over.

Imagine perceiving that the wheel can stop and you can exit gracefully. That is perception. Let's delve into it a bit more, and I will show you how these two, both a limiting belief system and perception keep you stuck and unhappy.

Creating that new belief that can guide you to an original path for yourself is a little different than when I talk about how your perception is your reality.

For example, perception is, "I don't have any money. Therefore, I'm broke."

You must look at things differently.

"I can't get a job because I'm not smart enough. I don't have a college degree, and I can't get into college because I'm not smart. I don't have any money. I can't land that job because I'm not pretty enough, or I don't have the resume behind me."

These are all based on perception.

The perception is you can't do it. Now add a limiting belief system of "no one in my family or friends has ever done that" and you are on the hamster wheel I was talking about.

See how they tie in?

If you sit down and look closely at something, you can figure out how to do anything.

We have people that haven't even graduated high school building computers. We've seen that. We've seen people like Steve Jobs, Bill Gates, Rachel Ray, Mark Zuckerberg, and Michael Dell, who didn't finish college go on to do great things.

We've seen Ben and Jerry drop out of Penn State, my Alma Mater, and then they're bankrolling over ice cream. They made ice cream for God's sake. They made delicious ice cream, but they made ice cream. They came up with unique names and flavors that had not been done. AND they almost failed. Almost. They ran out of money, and their families told them it wouldn't work. Their limiting belief system tried to drag them back into the concept that they had to do what every kid in the neighborhood was doing, go to college.

They didn't. They made ice cream. People came from all over to buy it from their store. Their perception was they could do it, and it worked. It worked so well their ice cream is in almost every major food chain in America. They had a dream, and they went for it. So, perception is their reality. If these school dropouts perceived they couldn't do it, they would not have. But they were able to create a different perception of reality.

What is your perception of your current situation? Do you feel stuck? Unhappy? Bored? Are you wondering if this is 'all there is to life'?

Well, Colonel Sanders started his KFC chicken chain in his 70's, and Morgan Freeman didn't act until his 50's. What are you waiting for?

Happiness won't fall in your lap.

The book won't write itself.

The company won't be created without you.

One thing my mother says to this day that drives me crazy is the word 'someday.' I ask if she wants to go on a trip, and it is 'someday.'

I hate someday. It is not a day of the week. Today is your 'someday.' What will you create once you tear down the limiting belief system and change your perception of a negative situation?

~

 **DO THIS:** Make a list of all the things your family told you that you could not or should not do. This is your Limiting Belief System. Now make a second list of all the things you think you can't do, this is your perception. Compare the two lists. These are the items that will hold you hostage from your dreams. Decide which items you need to change and which you need to let go. You can not hold on to archaic ideals and make waves.

~

*Best-selling author J. K. Rowling's life is a classic "rags to riches" tale, going from unemployed single mother "as poor as it is possible to be in modern Britain without being homeless" to one of the wealthiest women in Britain. Rowling describes herself before Harry Potter as being "the biggest failure I knew." Yet within her failure, she found liberation.*

*"I was set free because my greatest fear had been realized, and I was still alive, and I still had a daughter whom I adored, and I had an old type-*

*writer and a big idea. And so rock bottom became a solid foundation on which I rebuilt my life."*

*She sent her finished manuscript to 12 different publishers only to be rejected by them all. A Bloomsbury editor finally picked up the book for an advance of just £1,500. Her editor suggested she get a teaching job as it was unlikely that she would earn a living from writing children's books. The book went on to become one of the best-selling series in history, with over 450 million copies purchased worldwide.*

*Says Rowling, "It is impossible to live without failing at something unless you live so cautiously that you might as well not have lived at all - in which case, you fail by default."*

*Despite the rejections and failures, Rowling kept going. If she would've said, "I'm not smart enough, I'm not educated enough, I'm not a good enough writer," we would not have Harry Potter. She believed in herself and what she was doing.*

~

Perception is reality.

Let that ruminate for a minute.

Perception is reality.

If you perceive you are stuck, you will remain stuck. Once you realize you can create your reality, you will fly.

I know, I know, "what if I fail?" you just said it didn't you. You might fail, but what if you succeed?

See how your brain went right to the negative of you failing. It can't be done, and you can't possibly succeed. We will cover flying without a safety net in a later chapter; for now, we focus on creating the dream and changing your perception of the outcome.

We must look at our perception of any goal or situation. If we perceive we can't hit something, we won't. If we have understood that there is a "glass ceiling" or limit, there is, and we will be thwarted in our attempts to break it.

In my industry, the media dubbed me 'the female Dr. Drew.' If you don't know who he is, he is the pinnacle for addiction medicine. That means I hit the ceiling, and there is nowhere left to go. So, what did I do? I popped out a book about how to get through it. What's next? That is how you should be thinking.

We must be able to go beyond that glass ceiling to get where we want to go. How do we do that?

The first thing you do is figure out what your perception is, to identify how you are assessing a situation, and what forms your opinion or view.

Then you figure out, is it real, or is it not real?

For example, let's say my perception is, "I can't go to college because I'm not smart enough."

Well, is that real or not real? The reality is, if you did well enough in high school grade-wise, you could go to college.

If your perception is, "I can't afford it," then you start researching how you can afford it. There are grants, programs, and funding sources you don't know about that are available, specifically for people just like you.

I started in community college because I couldn't afford a state school and saved up to cover my first semester at Penn State. Then I got my Master's Degree for FREE by doing an assistantship. I worked for West Chester University in the economics department in exchange for free tuition. Yes, FREE tuition. I didn't have the money for college, and my family was not helping (remember the limiting belief system that I was not supposed to go to college). I figured it out. I made it happen. If I would have allowed the limiting belief system to consume me (no one in our family goes to college) coupled with my perception (college is too expensive, and I can't afford it) I would never have thought outside the box and found a way to go.

My perception did not become my reality.

We must look at our perception first. Is it valid, or is it made up? We can also ask others close to us or ask in online groups or forums if anyone else has the same reading on a situation. The picture may change drastically based on the feedback you receive.

Then we need to look at our limiting belief system. What does our family say? And more importantly, what does our society say? Especially if we're starting to hear contradicting views or having some insights that make us question our previous take on specific situations or opportunities.

I feel most of the time, society says women should be able to cook, clean, and birth babies. In general, that's what society may tell us. But that doesn't necessarily mean that every woman must be able to do that.

I don't cook and clean, and I did not have any kids. Could I learn to cook and clean, sure, but it does not interest me. Running a company and writing a book does, so I find a partner that likes those domestic things, and it allows me to spend my time doing the things I love and not on the tasks I hate.

How did I do that?

When I was 34 and still single (remember I was career-focused, not family-minded) I decided I wanted to take a husband. I had a tall order. I wanted a husband that liked to cook and clean (not just could do it, but enjoyed it) and already had kids that were not living with him. I also wanted a partner that liked to travel and did not own any property (I didn't want to get stuck someplace). I also added to my 'perfect partner list' with a request of having fun, being an entertainer, and of course, tattoos. This was not in alignment with my family's values where the women are in the kitchen and the men in the tv room. It was my belief and value.

Not long after creating my list and putting it on paper all around the house (just like I talked about in my Money Chapter before) did my perfect partner appear. We meet in NYC at a Starbucks. He had every quality on the list, and by then I was telling each potential suitor upfront that I am a non-traditional woman. Most men were looking for the wife that cooked cleaned and provided children, and I did not want to sit through an entire meal if this was going nowhere. That was not me, and because my perception was, I could be anything I wanted to be, and I can have the perfect partner, I got it. He was elated that I would be the primary breadwinner and he could play music (he is a drummer in a rock band) and lounge by the pool. He loves to cook and makes 5-star meals. Not just grill, mind you, he actually can cook a steak filet or ahi tuna like a Le Bec fin chef.

My perception to create the perfect partner became my reality, but I had to break the limiting belief that I had to be the housewife first.

Does that make sense?

First, you have to break the limiting belief, and then you have to change your perception of what your reality is to what you want it to be.

We should ask ourselves, "Does society, my culture, or my community hold me back?" It's not just my Mom and Dad, not just my family system, but also what is my society telling me?

Society told me that as a woman, I should have kids. Society told me that as a woman, I should know how to feed my man. I believe there is a book from 1960 about how to be a good wife. My mother gave it to me as a wedding present as a joke. I did nothing on that list in the book. My sister can make home-made pasta for her husband while juggling a job, two kids, PTA duties, and making cupcakes. I had the fire department at my house last time I tried to cook, and the last time I 'borrowed someone's kids for the day" I lasted two hours with them before I sent them home.

Is her husband happy with her? Yes.

Is my husband with me? Yes.

Different perception.

Different realities.

The same family and the same limiting belief systems, I just changed mine to suit my needs.

We also need to ask ourselves, is society telling me, "I'm not good enough, I'm not smart enough, I'm not pretty enough?" What is society saying?

Once we have been able to answer these questions honestly, we can decide if this is an option we're going to explore to see if there are ways to work around these limiting beliefs and values.

~

**DO THIS**: Write down on paper the life you have (list it all) and the life you want to create. Maybe it is you work a job and want to work for yourself? Or you want to change your circle of friends. Whatever it is, write down what you have now and what you want to shoot for. Then focus on it. And be ready for the big changes.

~

Along with society, the other issue we must address is social media and its impact on our belief systems. This has proven to become a potent force in today's world.

Social media can hold us back. If we look at people's pictures on Facebook or Instagram and they are beautiful, we can say to ourselves, for example, "Well, I'm not as pretty as her, so I'm not going to apply to be a model."

Or "look at how thin she is, I will never look good in a bikini."

This creates what I would call a "skewed perception of reality" and is another limiting belief. It happens every day on social media and can have disastrous effects.

So not only do you have to battle your family's limiting beliefs and society's limiting beliefs, but you also have social media to tend to as well. I always say social media is not reality. People use filters and photoshop their photos. It is not real. Even worse, celebs use professional photographers to take a 'selfie.' No one looks like that in real life, I should know I work with celebrities for a living, and once the makeup and wigs come off, they look just like you and me.

Watching people post about their amazing vacations while you are cleaning baby puke off your shirt wishing you were in Cancun with them, can hinder your psyche. Your perception is that their life is amazing (it may not be, you just see the best parts) and their life is better and more fun than your life. That is not your reality, and it is theirs. You can change your perception of what you see and change your reality around it.

When you change your perception, you change your mood and your entire thinking process. Instead of being mad or envious of their Cancun vacation, try to be happy that they are going. Then get on the internet and look for great deals for yourself. Reach out and ask them who they used to book the trip. I see trips all the time that come through my social media feed for super cheap. I took an entire Vegas trip for $250 including air and hotel for four days. Look for what you need and make it a reality.

I once flew first class from Miami to Alaska and used points and didn't pay a penny for my trip. I posted a happy photo on Facebook and Instagram, and a few people were envious when I told them how I flew for free, they all started doing it. Not only did I use points on my Amex, but I also used my up-grades on American Air to get free first-class seats. I also upgraded my card to use the lounges at the airports (cost me $450 a year), and I eat for free when I fly. I usually spend $30 on food at the airport, and this gave me huge savings, but there is even more. I was able to do by researching and being crafty. Your perception can become your reality. You just need to put in the work. People that don't have a lot of money have time. Use it wisely and use it to get what you need.

~

**DO THIS:** Get on social media. What are your friends and colleagues posting? Where are they going, and what are they doing? Do they look happy? Do you want what they have? Start your research and write down your findings!

~

Another huge key to deciphering all of this is your thinking. Your old thought patterns are not going to help you create new experiences.

The key is change. Change your thinking. Change your pattern. Change your perception. Change your limiting belief system.

The most common mistake when it comes to limiting belief systems and changing patterns is to repeat the pattern that our parents taught us or what we were surrounded by while growing up.

In my case, it was my parents telling me I was not smart enough to go to college. Had I believed in that and followed their lead, I would have repeated the pattern. Fortunately, we can break the tendency to continue this way of thinking, and that's precisely what I did. And many others have done this too by refusing to listen to the naysayers and believing in themselves, not in what others were telling them.

We apply to get into a college, and instead of applying to multiple colleges, we apply to one or two, and if we get rejected, we are telling ourselves, "Well, I'm too stupid. I'm never going to go to college."

Which then reiterates that limiting belief system you possibly received from your parents just like I did.

The second biggest mistake I see far too often when it comes to limiting belief systems and perception, preventing them from becoming reality, is just giving up too quickly.

Far too many people never achieve their potential because they try it once, and it fails. Suddenly they're telling themselves, "Oh look, I'm not supposed to do that. I knew I wouldn't be able to do that, and my Mom was right, she said I would never get into that school."

My advice to you, obviously, is do not stop and give up because it didn't work the first time. The second time, the third time. I say it's the rule of nine. Try at least nine times.

Look how many times J.K. Rowling was rejected. Rowling's story isn't alone, Dr. Seuss was rejected 27 times before "lucking" into a publisher and Stephen King's first novel Carrie was thrown back at him an astonishing 30 times after he had denied it himself and tossed it in the trash (his wife had pulled it out and encouraged him to keep trying).

If you believe in yourself and your path, don't give up easily.

Now, I'm not saying repeating the same exact steps or actions that failed the first time. But if you want to go to college, maybe you start with community college first.

And when your grades are good enough, you begin applying and figuring out how to go to a state school. You don't have to go to Yale. You don't have to go to MIT, and you don't have to go to Brown.

I went to Penn State, but I went to community college first. I didn't go to a big college at the start because not only was I told I wasn't smart enough to go, I had no money to go. And then, when I sat down and thought about it, I realized I was smart enough to go, and that eliminated that belief. Then I figured out how to get a loan, and off I went.

Think about that. Not only was I told you don't go, you can't go, but we can't afford it. That's three different limiting belief systems I had to overcome and change my perception of how to do it. I didn't have the money to go at the time, and part of the limiting belief system with my family was, "You're not smart enough, and we can't afford it."

Had I believed that and bit into that, I wouldn't have gone to college. I focused on the "how I can" instead of the "no I can't" and was able to find a way to make it happen. Now I have a Ph.D.

Keep going until you figure out what you need to get, where you need to go, and how you are going to get there with a limiting belief system. We will talk more on the roadmap to how to make it happen.

I also want you to understand that you don't have to listen to society. How often do we hear society telling us that we're too fat? The message we hear is that women are supposed to look like Kim Kardashian or Brittney Spears, and at one point Twiggy was the look of the day.

You're either too fat, or your boobs are too small or too big. There's always something wrong with you according to society. Don't listen to Society.

A lot of these photos we are basing our societal values upon are doctored with software, they're not real.

Another societal "norm" we can break is the one where society says, "Women are supposed to clean and do the laundry." In my case, my husband cooks, cleans, and does the laundry, and I work. We have both eliminated the belief system that would say because I'm a woman, those are the things I should be doing, and he is the one who should be "bringing home the bacon."

When I used to get together with my girlfriends, they talked about what they cooked, what their husbands are doing or making, what laundry they did, where their kids are going. I didn't enjoy the times we spent together. It was hard for me to relate to them.

And since I don't have a frame of reference for all that Pinterest meal prep and who made homemade Christmas decorations, I felt lost in that world. I could have said, "Well, I guess I should cook, clean, do laundry, and make babies, and then I get to hang out with my friends." Instead, I chose to get a new group of friends.

Yes, I ditched my original tribe in favor of a new one that I fit. You have to find like-minded people, or you are in a cage, not a circle (just like I told you in the tribe chapter).

Your perception is your reality. My perception of my girlfriends was, "You're getting married and having babies and you cook and clean."

The perception would be that's what I do, but because it's a limiting belief system, I turned it around and said, "I don't need to do that. I'll find friends that do what I do."

This goes back and ties into the chapter about finding your tribe. You start to adopt the limiting belief system of your tribe. That means if you're in the tribe that says you can't, you shouldn't, or you won't, you then pick up the mentality of that tribe. We have to find a path to get around that. We must smash the glass ceiling and move forward and upward.

Are you ready to change your perception and get rid of your limiting belief system?

~

**DO THIS:** I want to hear some of your limiting beliefs, and how you plan on getting past them, how you are creating new beliefs. Go to www.UnpauseYourLife.com and grab your FREE PDF exercises!

 **DO THIS:** Make a list of all the limiting belief systems in your family right now and put a check-mark next to the ones that resonate with you. If it does not resonate with you, change the limiting belief to something that resonates with you.

 **DO THIS:** Write down your perception of your life you have right now. Write down what you want it to be. Make a list of roadblocks that stop you from having the life you want. Think of it as a quick street map. Detours and potholes. What can be avoided, and what can be created over, like a bridge over the potholes?

 **DO THIS:** Leave a legacy exercise: If you can write your own Wikipedia about yourself, what would it say? What would your Legacy entail? What would it say now, and what would you prefer it say?

# CHAPTER SIX

# FLYING WITHOUT
# A SAFETY NET

*When Do I Jump?*

We are going to cover the scariest part of this whole process, the one that trips almost everyone up and keeps them from moving forward into the life they want and deserve, blocking them from their purpose.

Are you ready to take the next step? Are you ready to have a kickass life and financial security? You spent the last few chapters learning how to find your purpose, find your tribe, and get in the money mindset; now it is time to get rolling!

Finding the courage to jump from a relatively comfortable job and spot can be what keeps many people stuck. Even if you are just barely scraping by and making enough money to live on, even if you can't stand your boss or what you do, it's easy to get caught up in a cycle and get complacent in your current situation.

A lot of fear is generated when you are about to try something new or are concerned about finances and not being successful. For me, I've always been more irritated by having a boss and working the traditional 9-5 jobs. I was bored, and of course, you hit the financial ceiling very quick. Even if you get a small raise, you are making them so much money, and you are the one doing all the work!

I quit my job as a therapist and a program director in treatment because I was making $42,000 with a Master's Degree, working on a Ph.D. and the owner who had no education beyond high school, pulled up in his top of the line Porche with an attitude everyday. His wife had a top of the line Mercedes (new one every six months) and every pair of red bottom shoes they make.

The owner would remark how successful he was, but in reality, he was only as successful as his staff. My bank account was always in the negative after I paid rent, car, school loans, food, and gas. I barely scraped by on that crappy salary. My coworkers were petrified to leave, how they would pay the rent was their big hang up.

I hated my job.

I hated the owner.

I hated my crappy salary.

I hated my 10-hour day.

I was the only one that could Jump, so I did.

I quit my job with $300 in my account.

Now, mind you, I quit my job on a condition. I did interview at other locations and had one job ready at $10,000 more than I was making, but it was a tad longer drive and not exactly what I had wanted. It had drawbacks. What I wanted was to have my own company again.

I walked in the door and told my husband that I was going to start there in two weeks, but if I could make more money in that two-week window than I would in my 30-day job, I was not going to take the new job.

Well, I got a surprised look followed by "how will we pay the rent in MIAMI" (think NYC rent prices).

In my usual fashion, I laughed and said: "watch what I create."

See, I have jumped before. In 2003 I packed everything I owned into my Ford Explorer and drove from West Chester, PA to Dallas, Texas. I had no job lined up, no income, and only a credit card to live off of that I could barely afford the monthly fee. One day my friend and I decided to start a fitness company. I flipped over the plastic bin I had kept my clothes in (we had not bought any furniture) and put my computer on it, sat on the floor, and that was my 'desk' for the next six months while we created The Motivators Network and National Home Trainers.

We made 150K the first year, 1.1 million the second, and 4.1 million the third year. We had offices in 4 states and an in-house staff of 17 in a penthouse on Commerce St. in Dallas, Texas, and over 1000 independent contractors around the USA.

I jumped.

I jumped hard and fast.

And it worked.

So, this time, I was ready to jump again. My husband though was worried and rightfully so. I was responsible for half the bills, what if I couldn't do it?

What if I failed and all the financial responsibility fell on his shoulders? He wasn't built to run a company, and he jumped before when he left home at 17 from Florida to Los Angeles to be a drummer in a rock band, and he made a career out of music. However, musicians are notoriously broke, so he had not jumped financially.

The conversation went like this (similar to what is probably going on inside your head)

What if you fail?

What if we are homeless?

What if we have to move in with one of our parents?

What if we fail?

Am I making the right decision?

Where is my business plan?

See...your brain is right there! All the negative thoughts from childhood, from your parents, from your negative self-talk, will manifest themselves in your head.

Jumping is not comfortable.

Change is not comfortable

To grow, we must be uncomfortable.

Anytime we grow, as individuals or as business owners, it's going to be uncomfortable. Nothing positive will come without some stumbles and challenges along the way. You will fall, you might even cause an avalanche, but if you truly pursue your passions, it will work.

If you know what you want to do and by now you should have a good idea, you can jump.

The dilemma of jumping is not new, and it is true for anyone. The Daymond Johns and Vera Wangs of the world have all faced obstacles they needed to overcome. They didn't back down, they figured it out, and they hustled.

What I've developed is not so much a "safety net" but a parachute. We can never be completely safe unless we don't do anything at all unless we sit on a couch without moving. Even then, we are compromising our health and letting life pass us by.

My mother's favorite word was 'someday.' She would always say, "someday I will visit you in Texas, someday I will take that trip." Yet, someday never came.

Someday is not a day of the week.

I understand it is nearly impossible to be risk-free; we can manage our risk and lower it by following some basic yet effective strategies.

I'm going to outline those strategies here, tried and true approaches to managing the risk that have worked for countless people in the past and will continue to keep working in the future.

Just remember, you will never reach your goals or find your definition of success without leaping from where you are today towards your desired destination.

Let's get you prepared to launch!

~

The first thing we're going to do is begin our preparation for our jump. We're going to start putting together our parachute and packing it up nicely, so it deploys perfectly when we do the jump.

I'm assuming you have a job now and can pay your bills. Now, if you have no income and no job, you need to figure out a stream of income and fast. It can be anything you love, and you need to focus on it. If you have a job, you can jump softly and test out the waters before you dive in. But if you are unemployed, you have no option but to jump.

I'm also going to hope you do not have so much debt that you cannot find a way to start saving some money. Now when I jumped, I was over $40k in student loan debt and over $25k in credit cards. It didn't stop me. I had nowhere to go but up.

Most people spend way too much, more than they make, which causes them to get sucked into a spiral of doom with too much debt and too little income.

I am not saying cut all corners, but look at where you spend your extra cash if you have it. If you are spending $5.00 a day on Starbucks 5 days a week, that is $100 a month right there and $1200 a year. Now I love my coffee, so for me, that was not an option to remove, but you can get creative. Make it at home, drink it at work, etc. If you are buying clothes and jewelry you already have and don't need, slow down on that.

Most financial experts say you need three months of income in your bank account to jump. I have done it on three months' salary, and I have done it on only $300, but I am the anomaly. If you jump, be prepared to hustle. Please don't jump with $300 and sit on the sofa waiting for your parachute to open, because it won't. You will need to work and work hard.

Society has conditioned you that you need the newest gadget, TV, phone, ring, shoes, or whatever to be 'happy.'

Truth is you don't.

If you know who you are and what direction you want to go, you will be happy. But you need to jump, and you need to hustle to make it happen.

You need the discipline to do what financial guru Dave Ramsey says, "You must live like no one else now... so later you can live, *and give*, like no one else."

~

 **DO THIS:** Make a list of all your expenses. Where are you over-spending, and where can you cut these expenses to put towards your dreams? Start a new bank account where you can save or have these extras pulled out of your check and deposited elsewhere. But first, find them.

Alright, so you're making money and spending wisely, and what I want you to do to start sewing up your parachute is to save just a bit of money.

Do it consistently. You can have it drawn out of your account automatically if needed, but this needs to be a weekly or even daily habit.

Make it a game, a bit of a challenge to see how much money you can save every week or even every day.

~

I recommend saving up at least three months of expenses before any jump if you are a little more comfortable with risk. But I want you to make your cutoff a maximum of six months of expenses in the bank, then jump.

I know that probably sounds frightening as hell for some of you right now because there are a lot of you out there who need to have everything planned out, every detail.

And then there are others, like me, who will jump into anything and know they are going to fall and scrape a knee, but they will jump up and say, "I'm okay! That didn't work; I'm going to try this... Oops! That didn't work either; I better try this instead."

These people are fewer in number, mainly because of how we are trained, how we are raised, and "protected" by our parents in many cases. When you look at little kids who are learning to walk or ride a bike they fall, sometimes a lot, and they get all banged up. But they get back up and keep trying until they get it right until it becomes effortless.

Remember how I told you I came home and told my husband I was going to try my private practice out, and if I can make a month's pay in 2 weeks, I would not take that job?

Well, I did it.

That day I printed up business cards and put some at the local gym and the local vitamin store. My phone rang 5 hours later for an appointment. I met the guy the next day, and I sold him for ten sessions of coaching. I spent the rest of the day traveling all over and placing business cards at Starbucks, rest areas, gas stations, etc. and the phone rang two days later with another client. I had hit my goal and even went over in less than five days.

I had made more than a month's pay that fast, and it cost me a tank of gas and $25 for business cards.

I never took the second job.

My husband was stunned.

I jumped, I lept, and I landed.

BUT... I hustled to make it happen.

This level of determination is the attitude you want to adopt for jumping into your new passion and purpose. It will be a little bumpy at first, but it will get better and easier, I assure you.

Then I went a full week with no new clients, no calls, nothing. I got discouraged.

Then another week with nothing. I was starting to panic. You cannot create abundance in a panicked state. You focus, you get out the vision board (check out the next chapter), and you create, and you focus, and you create and focus.

Then you strategize, and you hustle.

You network, and you hustle.

I called and emailed everyone I knew and told them what I was doing.

The phone rang that day, and I signed up two more clients.

When you jump, the first thing that happens is the Universe will throw a test your way, something you are not expecting. Those who try to plan it all out struggle even more because of these unexpected wrenches in the system. You can't plan it all out, life has a certain amount of chaos built-in, and you can forecast things, but you can't predict everything.

This test is all about how you will react, and if you're living in your purpose and passion, the test won't matter because you'll weather your way through. You'll see it for exactly what it is, which is a learning experience, not a problem.

I could have quit and gone back to a job, but I didn't. I stuck it out and kept going. This is where that little bit of extra cash in the bank account can help you feel safer. If you need it, plan it and keep it there so you can jump without feeling panicked.

Whatever challenge you get hit with, solve it, or decide it is not with the energy and move to the next thing.

The key is to keep moving.

I have seen so many people give up their dream because the beginning challenge was too hard, too long, or too frustrating.

Once you solve this challenge and learn from it, you'll move on to the next thing... and the next. Life is one big series of challenges, one after another, and you can choose the challenges. Put the ones in front of yourself that will lead you to your passion and purpose. Solve them, and you will eventually find your path.

~

People ask me if it is a good idea to start with a side gig or "hustle" before making the full leap. Maybe their parachute isn't quite ready, maybe they want to test the waters to help determine their path, or maybe they need the extra income to speed up the process of launching.

Yes! It's a great idea and can help reduce the risk involved with your leap.

I have done this myself. I put up a basic website, and I said, "Okay, I'm going to see what happens."

I made a few phone calls, and I leveraged the power of social media. You can start a side hustle on social media like there's no tomorrow.

You can test your idea out, see if there is interest in what you want to offer and see how people react to what you are doing.

You can start small by messaging certain friends or put up a post telling people what you are trying to sell, your services or your product. You can get their feedback, ask them for referrals, and your goal does not have to be making a lot of money. When starting, you want to be serving at a high level, getting feedback on your products or services, gathering testimonials, and dialing in your offer.

You don't have to invest a lot of money, and I hear this often is a big stumbling block for people.

If you have a smartphone, you've got more computing power in your pocket right now than they used to land astronauts on the moon. You can connect with anyone, anywhere through your social media and you can start small. In my case, I had no overhead. I worked from home, so I didn't have an office. I didn't have any staff, and I used my cell phone, which I was paying for anyway.

The only investment I had was time and a few dollars for some basic business cards. And to be honest, you don't even need business cards.

Committing to a plan of action and preparing to jump, then leaping, is where the rubber is going to meet the road, and where most people drop off.

What does this look like for you?

What is your idea that you have to jump with?

Does it solve a pain point for people?

Does it make you happy?

What holds you back?

Answer those questions above, right now, right here. Get a pen and write, write, write!

~

*There's a 28-year-old at the front desk of my building who tells me he wants to open a coffee shop.*

*"That's my dream," he says to me.*

*I ask him, "You want to open a coffee shop and you're the front desk guy telling everyone, "Good morning! Here's your package!" ...why are you not opening a coffee shop?"*

*"It's so much work and money," he replies.*

*I looked at him, "Why don't you find investors?"*

*"It's not that easy," he says.*

*I tell him, "Yes, it is, it's all in your mindset."*

*"Where do I find investors?"*

*I explain that I'm going to a networking event that will have investors that evening and invite him to come with me, it's two blocks away.*

*"What time?" he asks.*

*I tell him it's at six, and he then lets me know, "That's right in the dinner hour."*

*"You don't want to open a coffee shop?" I inquire.*

*"Yes, I do," he says.*

*And I said, "So, is there a reason why you can't go to a free event where you could find an investor, and it's only two blocks away?"*

*He just stood there, staring at me.*

*I went on, "So, you don't really want to open a coffee shop. You talk about opening a coffee shop, but you like being a front desk guy telling people how good the morning is and that they have a package."*

*He stared some more, then asked, "Do you do this for a living?"*

*"Yeah," I said. "And I am damn good at it."*

*He's not ready to jump because his purpose is not in alignment with what he is telling me.*

~

Another huge hurdle many encounter is trying to decide on a business, what to do. This dilemma can get someone stuck because they want to start with their dream business, the "one" that's going to define their purpose.

Too often, people have this unrealistic expectation that the business or passion has to look a certain way. They spend more time working on planning than actually doing the execution of the project.

For example, my trainer has been talking about his girlfriend, who has been creating a food line for months. Naturally, being a foodie, I am hounding him for snacks every day we train. There is always an excuse as to why she doesn't have samples to promote her company. The biggest one was that she needed a specific container to provide the food. This was a stall tactic as not to get the business going.

Waiting on specific containers can be considered branding and marketing; however, if you have a potential sale or a potential client that is ready to sample and buy and you stall, you lose the sale, the deal, or the exact thing you are trying to create.

She should have jumped.

I would have purchased her service.

After three months of waiting, I found another service that has exceeded my expectations. She lost a customer because she was too afraid just to jump.

Just start with something. Anything.

You can change it as you go, you can add to it, it will morph into what you need and what you want. You may find that what you had originally envisioned or wanted has changed as well. Maybe your original plan needs a slight tweak or adjustment, so make it! You are not stuck in the original plan if it is not working. That is the beauty of the jump. You can jump and then fly and jump again.

The key is to start with *something* because whatever it is will likely change, evolve, or become something different down the road.

I recommend writing down ten business or passion ideas. Try doing a bunch of "brainstorming" either by yourself or with friends and family. Nothing is too crazy, write them all down.

Then, you're going to see what resonates with your gut based on your strongest feelings. What resonates the most? What feels great? Trust your gut. Remember, you can add more of these as you go. I started with addiction coaching and created the largest school for addiction studies in the world. As of this print, we are in 25 countries and five languages. We have 30 plus teachers and 30 plus classes. When I started in 2012, it was just coaching, and it was just me. We have a full staff now because I added and added and added.

But I jumped first with one idea.

Then I jumped with more ideas.

Not every idea worked, but those that did I ran with them, and you can do.

Take that top idea (or two) and do some research to see if there is a viable market for your product or service.

And if you find a bunch of competition, that's a good thing! That means there is a market. Do not try to come up with a business idea for something completely innovative and new. We're trying to be successful here, so you want something that has already been proven, you're just going to put your unique spin on it, your secret sauce.

Remember we covered figuring out who you are and what your passion is in life, now we implement these things and get working on it.

Grab a pen and paper and answer these questions. I don't care if you use a napkin or write in this book, jot some notes down.

What is the plan?

How much cash do you need to start this?

Do you need an investor?

Do you need office space?

If you are following a passion, do you need income, or can you jump?

How soon until you can launch?

Any pitfalls on this plan?

What is my niche market?

What can I do better than everyone else?

Next up, you hone the elevator pitch you have been working on. Whether you are pitching investors, family, funders, or right to the sale and prospects (most serviced-based businesses go right there), you need a great 30-second pitch. You need to hone your "elevator pitch" and the messaging and practice pitching it to your friends, family, at networking events, on your business card which you are leaving everywhere. This pitch is so important as it defines what you are offering, and you need to be clear. You can jump, but if you can't explain what you are doing, you will fail.

Get clear and concise on what you are doing, and what you want, then you jump, and you fly. Get the pitch down and ready.

Be ready to hear the word, 'No.' You will hear it and cannot quit or get discouraged. You can adjust your offerings and your price if necessary, but you cannot quit.

People are always going to say no, but you can't let somebody's opinion of you, or your business throw you off course.

It's a big world out there, and if you've chosen well, you don't need to sell a million copies of your product or land thousands of clients. You do, however, need to jump and start the process.

In the next chapter, you will learn how to manifest exactly what you want and create the roadmap to success you so desperately crave.

~

**DO THIS:** Head over to my site at www.UnpauseYourLife.com and check out our video series on how to create an elevator pitch that grabs the attention of your audience! Start with the script and tailor it to your passions and purpose!

~

*Entrepreneur and "Shark Tank" investor Daymond John had always wanted to run his own business.*

*Long before he made it big with the clothing line FUBU ("For Us By Us"), his entrepreneurialism started in the first grade.*

*He would take pencils and scrape the paint off, customizing them with the customer's name. His market was exclusively the prettiest girls in his class.*

*His parents divorced when he was 10, and from that point on, he was raised by his mom alone.*

*"I became the man of the house and started working at that age." He started working for $2 an hour, handing out flyers in his neighborhood of Hollis, Queens.*

*After scraping by in high school, he started waiting tables at Red Lobster in the early 1990s.*

*One day, his mom said, "Listen, you're going to have to figure out what you're doing the rest of your life, one way or another." He told her that he wanted to start an apparel company, so she taught him how to sew wool caps. He bought some cheap fabric, sewed 80 hats, and sold them for $10 each, John explained on a podcast with James Altucher.*

*"Did you go back the next day and sew more?" Altucher asked.*

*John responded: "No. I went back the next hour and sewed more."*

*After witnessing her son's plucky attitude and passion, John's mom mortgaged her home to raise some $100,000 to fund his business, which officially launched in 1992. He set up in her house, dividing his time between Red Lobster and FUBU. His brand took off after he got big names to wear his product in music videos, but he continued waiting tables.*

*John told Tim Ferriss. "To the public, FUBU was a huge company. Little did they know that I was still serving them shrimp and biscuits!*

*"At the point where I had enough money to quit, I decided that I had to give the business all of my attention and effort. So, I quit Red Lobster around '95 or '96 and went completely full-time with FUBU."*

*John's determination helped him turn a small operation based out of his mom's house into a thriving business with $350 million in revenue within six years.*

~

**DO THIS:** Join us at www.TheMoneyMasterMindClub.com if you are ready to jump! We have the tribe ready, the Mastermind Group and we meet weekly to discuss elevator pitches, plans, manifestation boards and more!

**DO THIS:** Not ready to jump? Go to www.UnpauseYourLife.com and download some of our FREE PDF templates to get you going!

**DO THIS:** Sit down and write your best case and worse case scenarios if you jump. Will you be homeless and broke? What is the worst that can happen?

**DO THIS:** Keep your notes from the above questions and expand on them. How will you get this done? What does it look like and how soon can you get to jumping?

**DO THIS:** Go ahead, get it out of your system. List everything that could go possibly wrong. All of it. Make the long list and get it out of your head. Now make the same list of what you really, really want. Make the shift happen.

# CHAPTER SEVEN

# CREATING A ROADMAP TO SUCCESS

## *What Is My Vision?*

We've reached the final piece of this amazing journey. Now that you have worked on building a foundation, done the groundwork for your new venture, discovered your purpose, found your tribe, made the jump, or at least thought about it, you need a plan. A real, viable plan.

That's what I call your "Roadmap." You must have a roadmap to success. You can't just go, "I want an Aston Martin" and sit on the sofa and manifest it into your world. You need to have a step-by-step plan. Law of Attraction only works if you implement it. Wanting it and writing it on your vision board is just the beginning; you need the plan to reach your goals.

Think of it a little like the Maps app on your phone. When you punch in your destination, the app works backward to find the path of least resistance until it reaches your current location. It tells you if there is a long delay and may route you around the obstacles. That is your map, and you need a Roadmap to navigate life.

To start building your Roadmap, we are going to get crystal clear on your destination, then work our route back from there. I want you to be able to envision where you want to go, complete with sights, sounds, smells, every little piece.

To do this, we are going to build a vision board. You may have done this in the past, but today, I'm going to have you do it a little differently.

Now, you can go all out and buy a huge piece of cardboard, a wipe board or you can get paper and pen, it doesn't matter. You need something you can look at every day and make changes to, as your direction may change.

~

 **DO THIS:** Follow these steps to create your Vision Board:

1. Get a big piece of project cardboard or a wipe board or paper and pen.
2. Pick up a few magazines or go to google and prepare to print some pictures of what you want and where you want to go.
3. If you prefer to draw or color, grab colored pencils or crayons. Get ready to create a badass vision board and roadmap.

~

This Vision Board is going to help you create your Roadmap. We must know how we are getting from point A to point B. Knowing your purpose is going to motivate you and drive you forward, but you have to know the direction you're going.

Next, you must be okay with making money and spending money.

People want to make all the money they can, and they're afraid to spend it on their business. Instead, they will make some money and quickly spend it on things they want, not necessarily the things they need. So, before you spend your cash on one more bracelet, purse, pair of shoes, or a fast car, spend it on your personal development. That is right! Invest in yourself. Hire a business coach, go to the networking event, go to the conference, hire a transformational coach, and get going. If you are stuck and want to Unpause Your Life head over to that site and let us help you get going with business coaching! We also have a video series that goes with this book to keep you moving along!

You must spend money on your business consistently and invest in your business. One of my favorite quotes is from Pitbull (my 305 brother). He says, "Scared Money don't Make Money." This means if you are afraid to invest and market and put yourself out there, you will not get your needs met.

When I wanted to get some press, I had to hire a public relations firm, and they were not cheap. I had to save for it, I had to plan my roadmap to make sure I had the extra funds each month, and it took me nearly a year after I started my company to make sure I could afford it. Once I did, and it paid off, it became a monthly part of my vision board and roadmap, and I was able to add more items on there.

The next stop on my roadmap, after some basic press and a few small clips on the web, I wanted to get on television. TV is not easy to break into, and even the most skilled and educated people never get their '15 minutes of fame'.

I was able to secure a few clips, an NBC special on channel 4 in NYC, and even a quick piece on CNN with Don Lemon. But then, nothing for years. I couldn't get my foot back in the door, and I was told I needed to have a book. A book would show I had authority in the addictions space and could hold my own. So, I added "write a book" on my vision board, and my roadmap made a detour.

Writing a book is not a quick, easy thing. You don't just sit down and pop out a book in a weekend, despite any of the online gurus telling you can do it in a few days. You can't, and it takes work, but for me, it was a necessary detour in my roadmap.

The book *I Married a Junkie* broke me onto KTLA in Los Angeles, and it was bigger than Good Morning America. It was strategic in my marketing plan and necessary to move forward. AND it was expensive to do and self-publish.

Did I make the money back in book sales? Hell no, the goal was not to make a lot of money from book sales. The goal was to use that book to position me in a way that would get me onto TV, and it did.

And once I did that, I've been on as an industry expert over six times and I'm going back again. Now I'm an expert on KTLA, but I had to spend the money to write the book to position me as an authority in my industry first.

Here's another "secret," the ultimate goal was not getting on TV; that milestone is ahead of another goal. Remember, you're creating the roadmap to success, whatever that is for you, whatever your vision is, and then working backward from that, right?

My goal is not being cute on television. I don't need to be on every TV show and every book in America, but I want a big bank account that I can help people from because it takes money to help people. That's my goal. I didn't want to be an influencer or a reality TV star like a lot of people in my industry.

To do that, I have to do things I don't enjoy. I hate going on TV, but I need to move along my Roadmap. I want to get on TV for that reason, but to be honest, I hate it. It's expensive. It's a process, and it's a lot of anxiety to do these TV appearances.

Flying to LA, renting a hotel, car or UBER, and of course hair and makeup. Each trip is an easy $2500, and there is no guarantee I will get a client or even a call out of it. I have done appearances and gotten zero clients, no calls. And then I have done appearances and gotten 30-100 calls in a matter of minutes. In the end, it is worth it, it is a time-intensive and expensive process, but it is on my roadmap, and it is working.

That's a part of my roadmap and part of my vision board. I have events every week I have to go for networking. I can't stand networking either. It's all high-profile people in Miami, and in Miami, they're all concerned with fake eyebrows, fake hair, fake eyelashes, breast implants, butt implants, expensive clothes, and expensive cars.

I don't fit in.

I am as authentic as they come, and nothing is fake, and I have not had any work done yet. So, it is very uncomfortable to do these events, and yet I must. It is part of my roadmap, once I could hire staff, I assigned them the task of going to the events, but it was necessary at the beginning to get where I needed to go. Sometimes we have to buckle down and get it done, to get where we want to go,

I'm perfectly happy in my pajamas and my workout clothes. When I am working with clients via phone or teaching a seminar online, I am in my workout gear. I am comfortable, and part of my vision board when I was 14 was to work from anywhere via phone and laptop and wear comfy clothes. I was able to hone my roadmap over and over to get it where I needed it to be.

I don't even have an office.

I work solely by phone and skype, and I can travel to them or meet them in Miami at their hotel. All of that was on my vision board. Did it start that way? No. I had a job at one time, and I hated it. The old 830-5 and rush hour traffic going both ways, limited time for lunch, working 60 hours for 42K. I started there and then I quit, I needed a better life. I had to create a roadmap, and I had to figure out the next steps.

The next steps included a client, then an office, and then once I was established, I decided I hated the office and let it go and guess what? I got more clients.

Then I decided I wanted to travel and moved into a motorcoach RV and traveled for a year. You would think that by giving up my office, my idea of private practice, that my leads and clients would dry up, but no, as I was living my purpose and my truth, the Universe (or God, or whatever you call it) allowed me to enjoy myself, travel and my client list increased. I was living my best life, I was happy, and I was creating.

Part of your roadmap is getting over your hurdles, getting over your anxiety and your fear knowing what you need to do to get there, and every step along the path.

The other part is living your truth and passion. If you love what you do, really, really, really love what you do, the money will follow. You cannot dread getting out of bed and expect to create a fun and financially secure future.

But first, you must build the vision board and the roadmap to success.

Get that project cardboard, whiteboard or pad, and pen, and get ready to create. It doesn't have to be big, but something you can put where you will see it multiple times each day.

Not only will we create the roadmap, but we also need to create the vision and the mantras to keep you on track. Get a message up on the board to start or on your paper pad. Write it nice and big.

Then, I want you to add to your message on that board every day.

Make it positive and inviting.

It can be anything

"Money flies at me from all directions."

"I will be happy today."

Another thing I do on my board every month is to put a number up there that I want to hit for income. We hit it pretty much every month because that's what I focus on. Every day I focus on it when I wake up, and I go through all my mantras on the board and review the vision board to see if I need to add anything or I can cross anything off because it is completed.

Routine is key. Look at it every day, focus every day, even when the day is rough or tough or going in the wrong direction, you need to stay the course.

You can alter the roadmap; you can add and delete items on the board, but you must create.

Again, the point I want to stress is that it's not all fun and games. There's work involved, and that's where you have to have the discipline to stay on your roadmap.

Think of it this way. You get behind the wheel of a car. You go, and you buy the best car in the market, the nicest car. Or maybe you spend a quarter-million dollars on an RV, you get behind the wheel of the RV, and you want to go from Miami to LA. but you don't put gas in the tank, what's going to happen? You're not getting out of the driveway.

Then you sit there and complain you spent all this money on this, and you can't drive, and you can't do all these things, but you haven't done anything to get there. Maybe you entered the address in the GPS to get it pointed in the direction of LA. There are going to be tolls, you have to have toll money for each toll you go through, and you have to have gas in the tank, you have to have food, what are you going to do for food?

So, there is pre-planning, and there is setting it up. Otherwise, it is a disaster. Common mistakes are that people don't plan far enough ahead or they don't plan at all, and they're just living by serendipity. They think things are going to happen the way they should happen, but they don't take any action, and they don't plan.

Or, maybe they execute on only half of their plan. They might put gas in the RV, but they might not put the GPS on and just hope they get to LA. Or they don't anticipate potholes or road closures, and they don't have a plan to go around a road closure. Fear and uncertainty kick in, and they sit there, or they give up and abandon the RV and walk home.

You should always have something else on the table. What else are you working on? Multiple streams of income are also key if you are trying to build a business. I don't just have a coaching company. I have coaching. I have classes. I have a book that I wrote, and you are reading it. There is a video course to go with the book to dive deeper and get more clarity (Head over to www.UnpauseYourLife.com to check out the video series!). I am always thinking of what I can add and what I can tweak and what is working.

I'm doing all these different things. I'm making money by renting my RV. Who would've thought to do that? I have a house in Colorado that I'm renting out. All these things are these multiple streams of income, and it creates some cushion, "insurance" so to speak.

You may have heard the phrase, "Don't put all of your eggs in one basket." That's what they are referencing because if you drop that basket, you are in a world of hurt. Best to have some eggs somewhere else, in a different basket.

But for now, let's get you one basket, one roadmap, and you can add all your ideas on it, and let's get a direction to go to each one.

One last thought before I end this chapter. Successful people tell themselves these four things daily:

1. I will figure it out.
2. Work hard to know what you don't know.
3. Never forget why you started.
4. No mistakes, only lessons.

~

**DO THIS:** Please go to www.UnpauseYourLife.com for more ideas on getting your Roadmap off the ground!

- Your Vision Board
- Your Ultimate Goal
- Your basic Roadmap outline. You are "here," and you want to go "there" and what are all the steps in the middle.

**DO THIS:** Go to Google or grab your magazines and scissors. Look for all the things you want to have first.

Cars, homes, wedding, partner, dog, kids, etc. cut them out of the magazine or google and print. Get them up on your vision board. This is your lifestyle vision board.

Next up your business/passion vision board. Keep creating and adding to your Roadmap to success!

# CONGRATULATIONS!

I am proud of you for making it this far! This shows me you have committed to changing your life for the better and moving forward towards the life you deserve!

If you haven't done it yet, head over to www.UnpauseYourLife.com to download your FREEBIES found there to get you moving in the right direction. Need more? Sign up for the video creation seies to get going on your newfound passion and purpose in life! Learn how to create an elevator pitch, build a brand, start to market and create that roadmap first hand!

Ready to rock?

Head over to TheMoneyMastermindClub.com and join our tribe of weekly mastermind calls, check out our business coaching and events that you can attend to learn more and get more involved!

Check out the video series and get serious about creating your goals! Join the tribe to hone ideas and network or get more business advise with the coaching packages!

And as always if you want to speak to a HUMAN call us at 800 706 0318 ext 1!!!

# ABOUT THE AUTHOR

Dr. Cali Estes, Ph.D., ICADC, MCAP, MAC CPT, CYT #1 Best Selling Author, plus a highly sought-after Celebrity Coach, Counselor, Life Coach, Transformational Coach, and Wellness Guru that blends talk therapy with forward and positive change to assist her clients in unlocking their true potential. She offers a unique service of combining holistic modalities with talk therapy that gets to the Root Cause of the issues you are experiencing and helps you simply "Unpause Your Life."

Named 'The Female Dr. Drew," by the media on the red carpet and one of '99 Limit Breaking Disrupter Females' by the Huffington Post, Dr. Cali Estes has helped CEO's, top musicians, actors, and entrepreneurs break the barriers that hold them back from life and achieving their goals and dreams.

Dr. Cali is known as the 'Battery Recharger' and is one of the top Transformational Coaches that can assist you in achieving your dreams and goals and breaking barriers.

Dr. Estes has over 25 years' experience working with clients that want to 'UnPause their life and Unpack their Backpack' to combat issues and behaviors that keep you 'stuck' in life and limit your goals and dreams in both your career and personal life.

Dr. Estes is an interactive, solution-focused Positive Psychologist and Cognitive Behavioral Therapist. Her unique no-nonsense approach of cognitive behavioral therapy, positive psychology, and life coaching, combine to provide the perfect support for anyone that feels stuck in life or a slave to an addiction/vice or bad behavioral that is ruining their life or simply wants to have a breakthrough in a limiting belief system. She has created several unique programs that are highly successful including; Sober on Demand, LaunchpadXpress, Progressive Leadership Platforms, and the 7Keys 'To tap into the wealth inside you' series. These unique programs have been proven to assist her clients in unlocking their full potential.

Dr. Cali Estes is a #1 Best Selling Author on Amazon has been featured on CNN, NBC, CNBC, CBS, FOX News, LA Times, Yahoo! News, Philadelphia Inquirer, Reader's Digest, MSN Money, Entrepreneur Magazine, People Magazine, Max Sports and Fitness, San Jose Mercury, The Fix, Dr. Drew, People Magazine, Washington Post, Yoga

Digest, and more. She was also featured in a riveting documentary about addiction, Gone Too Soon: The Story of Emily Cooley. She is also the host of the wildly successful 'UnPause Your Life' podcast.

Dr. Estes holds a Ph.D. from DSU in Psychology and Life Coaching, a Master's Degree from WCU, and an undergraduate from PSU, International Certification as a Drug and Alcohol Counselor, Master Certified Addictions Professional, as well as 24 certifications and over 20 years of experience as a Personal Trainer, Yoga Teacher, Pilates Teacher, Food Addictions Specialist and Life Coach. Her unique approach to get to the root cause of the problem with each client and relate on a humanistic level makes her desirable in this industry. She is also Founder and CEO of the largest addiction coaching school, with over 20 classes, 25 teachers and in 25 countries and translated into 5 languages.

More info: www.CaliEstes.com and
TheMoneyMastermindClub.com

Made in USA - North Chelmsford, MA
1053964_9781732178137
03.17.2020 1503